THE ABUSE ALGORITHM

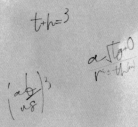

$t+h=3$

$\left(\dfrac{a\,b}{us}\right)^3$

$a\sqrt{tg}=0$
$r^2=th\text{/}m$

THE
ABUSE
ALGORITHM

LESSONS IN PROTECTING CHILDREN
FROM SEXUAL ABUSE

$t+h=3$

$\left(\dfrac{a\,b}{us}\right)^3$

$a\sqrt{tg}=0$
$r^2=th\text{/}m$

SHAVONTANA "STARR" DAVIS, ESQ.

THE ABUSE ALGORITHM

Lessons in Protecting Children from Sexual Abuse

Shavontana "Starr" Davis

NEW DEGREE PRESS

COPYRIGHT © 2021 SHAVONTANA "STARR" DAVIS

THE ABUSE ALGORITHM

Lessons in Protecting Children from Sexual Abuse

ISBN

978-1-63730-833-2 *Paperback*
978-1-63730-895-0 *Kindle Ebook*
978-1-63730-955-1 *Digital Ebook*

Dear Young Starr,

I wrote this book for you once I realized the significance of your plight. After Grandma taught you the power of choosing joy and modeled faith in action, your faith in God never wavered. You made it, baby girl. I'm proud of you.

To Grandma, my angel.

To Momma, my rock.

To Daddy, for showing me how I should be treated.

To Shelia for introducing me to Christ.

To Tank, TyDerrick, Ayanna, and Jamal for always showing up for me.

To Kia for protecting me as best as a child could.

To Devin for loving me through my pain.

To David and Parker, my greatest accomplishments.

To every survivor, known and unknown, you are not alone. I see you. I love you.

This book is dedicated to you.

CONTENTS

———

"*I am not working to educate, engage, and empower youth and the community about child sexual abuse and exploitation from a place of passion but one of purpose.*"

—SHAVONTANA "STARR" DAVIS

INTRODUCTION

—

"America seems filled with violent people who like causing people pain but hate when those people tell them that pain hurts."

—KIESE LAYMON

Ciera is a fifteen-year-old girl. She lives with her grandmother. Ciera's enrolled in school and goes most days. She enjoys singing, hanging out with her friends, and she loves Takis chips. Ciera also has sex for money, clothes, and food.

Neither of Ciera's parents are a part of her life. Her grandmother provides for her as best as she can on a fixed income, but her health is failing. Ciera's learned a lot about life on her own, without guidance from a trusted adult. She's never known a "safe space," and no one taught her how to protect herself. The truth is, Ciera's life represents the lives of many young women and men, mine included.

We don't even talk about the fact that we don't talk about it. Yet many terms are used to describe the main topic of this book—most of them sterilized for public consumption. The topic is child sexual abuse (CSA). And it is an all-too-common, widespread issue. One in ten children will be the victim of sexual abuse before their eighteenth birthday. In a typical American classroom, that means, on average, three of those precious souls will be robbed of their innocence before they graduate from high school. An estimated forty-two million adult survivors of CSA live in the United States. Without question, CSA is one of the most prevalent public health issues plaguing society.

Unfortunately, societal recognition of this well-documented issue is quite often trivialized as something that happens to "them." A common misperception about CSA is that it is a rare event perpetrated against girls by male strangers in poor, inner-city areas. On the contrary, CSA results in harm to millions of children—boys and girls alike—in large and small communities and across a range of cultures and socioeconomic backgrounds. These acts are perpetrated by many types of offenders, including men and women, strangers, trusted friends or family, and people of all sexual orientations, socioeconomic classes, and cultural backgrounds.

One thing most every child's situation shares is silence.

What is child sexual abuse?

According to Darkness to Light, an organization committed to empowering adults to prevent child sexual abuse, CSA is "any sexual act between an adult and a minor or between two minors when one exerts power over the other." It also includes non-contact acts such as exhibitionism, exposure to pornography, and voyeurism.

What the numbers say about CSA?

From 2009 to 2013, Child Protective Services agencies substantiated—or found strong evidence to indicate—that sixty-three thousand children per year were victims of sexual abuse. The majority of child victims are twelve to seventeen years of age. Of victims under the age of eighteen, 34 percent of victims of sexual assault and rape are under age twelve, and 66 percent of victims of sexual assault and rape are ages twelve to seventeen.

Who's committing this heinous crime, CSA?

Sadly, over 90 percent of the time, children are abused by someone they know and trust, including relatives. People with whom they share space and community. The impact of CSA can be far-reaching well into adulthood and affects the victim's physical, mental, and emotional health. Keep in mind this abuse exists in the dark and is not talked about. That lends incredible difficulty to accurately noting statistics. These numbers may only be the "tip of the iceberg" and all the more reason to bring CSA into the light. CSA often spans generations but more on that later.

What is Commercial Sexual Exploitation of Children (CSEC), or child sex trafficking?

CSEC occurs when someone causes a child to commit a commercial sex act. A commercial sex act is prostitution, pornography, or sexual performance done in exchange for anything of value, such as money, drugs, food, shelter, or clothing.

What the numbers say about CSEC?

According to Shared Hope International, the common age a child enters sex trafficking is fourteen to sixteen. CSEC is often viewed as "different" from CSA. Most don't consider the two to be the same, but CSEC is one form of CSA. The National Institute of Justice estimates that 70 to 90 percent of children commercially exploited were sexually abused first.

Who's committing this heinous crime, CSEC?

Many victims of CSA and CSEC live at home and attend school. In the US, many children are sexually exploited by their families or family friends for profit. Despite the sexual abuse, these children interact with educators, youth-serving professionals, and the community. Which means these adults have opportunities to help a child find their voice.

Awareness and prevention education are essential to protecting children and youth.

I grew up learning a mix of "stranger danger" and Drug Abuse Resistance Education (DARE), sprinkled with a dash of "good touch"/"bad touch." The education was surface level at best. It focused solely on how a child's negative behavior could result in serious, harmful consequences. No one prepared us for when kids the same age, older kids, or adults' negative behavior toward us resulted in serious, harmful consequences. They definitely didn't prepare us for those we trusted abusing us.

A victim knows their abuser over 90 percent of the time, yet we spend all this time educating our kids on strangers and how to avoid those bad people. How might the lives of the Cieras of the world have differed if she/he/they had had different conversations in their home- and school-life growing up?

Fed up with the normalization and causal acceptance of child victimization, I fully leaned into my calling. I am not working to educate, engage, and empower youth and the community about CSA and exploitation from a place of passion but one of purpose.

My life forever changed at seven. At seven, my molestation began, and my mom became addicted to drugs. I bounced around from house to house of different family members before finally moving in with Grandma the summer before sixth grade.

I lived with Grandma until I graduated from high school. Grandma was my person. My safe haven. She loved and supported me. She held me accountable. She planted seeds of love, compassion, understanding, trust, and the love of God in me through our relationship. I regularly prayed, "God, please don't take Grandma away from me." All I knew was that God didn't always give us what we wanted, but He always gave us what we needed. And, He knew I needed Grandma.

As close as we were, I still could not bring myself to tell her about the abuse. A confused child, I didn't tell anyone except my best friend, Kia. I made her promise to keep my secret. She did. But some secrets aren't meant to be kept. Because of the complex trauma experienced in childhood, I still battle with bouts of dissociation and repression. Yet, I vividly remember the night I confided in Kia. We'd grown close, inseparable even. It was rare that you saw one of us without the other. The summer before sixth grade cemented our friendship, our sisterhood.

One night I was sleeping over at her house. Instinctively, I believe her parents knew I was running from something, so they opened their home and hearts to me. We were in her bunk bed. It was white, with the twin-size bed up top and the full-size bed underneath. We were on the bottom bunk. I was closest to the wall, which is how I slept with Grandma. We were on our backs, staring into the darkness, talking about everything and nothing. In a brief moment of silence, it just kind of tumbled out.

I don't remember my exact words, but I remember how I felt. I told her through tears. Without warning, the dam broke. I was drowning in pain, shame, guilt, and anxiety. Even at that moment, I could not comprehend the toll of my silence. I was inconsolable. Yet, I knew the next day, nothing about my situation would change. But Kia and I were forever changed, an unspoken bond forged.

For the first time, in 2020, of all years, Kia and I talked about how she became my protector that night. How we were two kids weighed down by the woes of an all-too-common occurrence. Neither of us deserved the weight, but we carried it in stride, not as a badge of honor but as a reminder. In that very dark moment, I vowed when we got older, I would help girls like me.

The Starr Institute, Inc. (TSI) is me being to youth, girls, and boys, what Grandma was to me. I founded TSI in 2017 after overcoming CSA and having represented adult and minor victims of sexual abuse and exploitation in the criminal and juvenile justice systems. We educate, engage, and empower youth and the community about CSA and exploitation. We offer in person and virtual workshops that are interactive, culturally relevant, age-appropriate, and fun for youth ages twelve to seventeen. We offer training for adults and professionals too. My Safety Starts with Me is how TSI envisions our youth actively taking ownership of their safety. It's a movement. It's where we welcome youth to connect, apply the information we give them, share it with their friends and family, and become a part of our community.

Because Grandma was my person, I've always said if a child has *one* person who loves, supports, and holds them accountable, it makes all the difference. Imagine my surprise when I learned of a report from the National Scientific Council on the Developing Child, a multidisciplinary collaboration chaired by Harvard's Jack Shonkoff, that the power of that one strong adult relationship is a key ingredient in resilience.

What is resilience? A positive, adaptive response in the face of significant adversity.

Have you ever wondered why, when confronted with childhood trauma, some children adapt and overcome, and others bear lifelong scars that thwart their potential? A growing body of evidence suggests one common answer. Every child who winds up doing well has had at least one stable and committed relationship with a supportive adult. Many children and youth lack that meaningful relationship, and that's where TSI steps in.

This book, as Kia says, is me "finally making good on my promise."

The Abuse Algorithm shares the stories of CSA survivors, explores how Adverse Childhood Experiences (ACEs) impacted our lives, and how this all-too-common, widespread issue is a treatable public health crisis. CSA affects us all: survivors, those close to them, and the community. This book is for survivors and their loved ones, parents, caring adults, youth-serving organizations, and professionals.

An algorithm is a set of instructions designed to perform a specific task. The order in which steps are given can make a big difference. Using the experiences of each survivor, I'll highlight this process in an effort to deconstruct the antiquated societal perception of victimization and the misguided beliefs surrounding it. I'll also identify similarities between each survivor's story and my own. Don't get bogged down by chapter names. They are actual algorithms or data processing systems that coincide with each person's story and is an example of that algorithm of abuse.

Treat this book as a resource guide. Read it from cover to cover with the understanding that it's an uncomfortable read, yet a necessary one. Carefully consider the difficult topics that will be discussed. Continue your education. Pledge to utilize this tool to become a trusted adult who will listen to young people, understand their needs, and meet them where they are. I believe as we make awareness and prevention a priority and not just a reactionary response to an outcry, we will be in a better position to protect our children and youth from CSA and exploitation.

Sexual trauma is a heavy generational inheritance to carry, yet somehow many of us refuse to work on ways to prevent it. The silence, which ultimately protects perpetrators, serves no one and keeps us in a vicious cycle of pain.

Toni Morrison said, "… if you are free, you need to free somebody else. If you have some power, then your job is to empower somebody else."

A survivor's journey to healing is equivalent to that of an addict's recovery. Every day we make a choice. We choose to love ourselves, to see our value, to know that it wasn't our fault and that we are not defined by our pain. I found my voice. I speak for the survivors who cannot or do not wish to speak. It's their choice. But I will not stay silent so society can stay comfortable.

CHAPTER 1

ADVERSE CHILDHOOD EXPERIENCES

———

Dr. Robert Block, former president of the American Academy of Pediatrics, is known for saying adverse childhood experiences are the single greatest unaddressed public health threat facing our nation today.

In 2014, Dr. Burke Harris delivered a dynamic talk at a TED event titled TEDMED in San Francisco. Her talk, "How Childhood Trauma Affects Health Across a Lifetime," garnered over 7.2 million views on TED.com. Dr. Burke Harris was deliberate with her words. She boldly professed, "What I had thought of as simply best clinical practices, I now understand to be a movement. We marginalize the issue because it does apply to us. We don't want to look at it. We'd rather be sick. This is treatable. This is beatable. We need the courage to look this problem in the face."

A revered pioneer in the treatment of toxic stress, California's first Surgeon General and the founder and former Chief Executive Officer of the Center for Youth Wellness, Dr. Burke

Harris, created a clinical model that recognizes the impact of adverse experiences on health and effectively treats toxic stress in children. Her efforts left an indelible impression on the lives of many children in the Bayview Hunters Point neighborhood in San Francisco and beyond. The multidisciplinary approach focuses on preventing and undoing the chemical, physiological and neurodevelopmental results of Adverse Childhood Experiences (ACEs). The Center for Youth Wellness integrates primary health care, mental health and wellness, research, policy, education, community and family support services to children and families.

Where did ACEs Come From?

Conducted between 1995 and 1997, the CDC-Kaiser Permanente ACE Study (Study) is one of the largest investigations of the intersections of childhood abuse and neglect and household challenges and later-life health and well-being. It asked 17,500 adults if during childhood they experienced physical, mental, emotional, or sexual abuse, physical or emotional neglect, parental mental illness, substance dependence, incarceration, parental separation, divorce, or domestic violence. The study's population was 70 percent Caucasian and 70 percent college educated.

Each time a person responded affirmatively, they received a point, and that point was compared against health outcomes. The research found that the long-term impact of ACEs determined future health risks, chronic disease, and premature death. Individuals who had experienced multiple ACEs also faced higher risks of depression, addiction, obesity, attempted suicide, mental health disorders, and other health concerns.

Dr. Burke Harris decided to pursue this harmful exposure immediately after a colleague presented her with the study. The findings are alarming but not surprising. According to Dr. Burke Harris, "Childhood trauma increases the risk for seven out of ten of the leading causes of death in the United States. In high doses, it affects brain development, the immune system, hormonal systems, and even the way our DNA is read and transcribed. Folks who are exposed in very high doses have triple the lifetime risk of heart disease and lung cancer and a twenty-year difference in life expectancy."

The Impact of ACEs:

Across fifty states, 50 percent of children's ACEs are acquired by the age of three.

If left untreated, children with a high ACE score face a twenty-year decrease in life expectancy.

Can you see now why I call this a public health crisis?

Physical and Behavioral Health

Children who experience four or more ACEs are 7.4 times as likely to suffer from alcoholism and 12.2 times as likely to attempt suicide.

Education

Children who experience two or more ACEs are nearly three times more likely to repeat a grade.

Criminal Justice

Juvenile offenders are four times more likely to have experienced four or more ACEs than those in the study.

Dr. Block and Dr. Burke Harris's words are a global call to action to us all. A number of strategies involve people from all sectors of society who can prevent ACEs from happening in the first place and lessen the harmful effects of ACEs that have already occurred. The harmful effects of ACEs can affect everyone in our communities, and everyone can be helpful in preventing them. By keeping ACEs from occurring in the first place and taking quick action when an ACE happens, communities can help all children and youth reach their full potential.

Ways to help prevent ACES:

- Strengthen families' financial stability

- Promote social norms that protect against violence

- Help kids to have a good start

- Teach healthy relationship skills

- Connect youth with caring adults and activities

- Intervene to lessen immediate and long-term harms

After examining the ACEs scores, researchers learned that:

- With an ACE score of four or more, an adult's risk of developing heart disease or cancer doubles

- With an ACE score of five or more, there's an eight-time greater chance of alcoholism

- With an ACE score of six or more, an adult will die on average twenty years earlier

I took the ACEs questionnaire and received a total of six points out of only a total of ten questions. About six in ten adults surveyed reported experiencing at least one ACE, and nearly one in six of them reported experiencing four or more different types of ACEs. The ACEs questionnaire is included in the resources section of this book. I encourage you to take it.

Trauma begets trauma if left untreated. ACEs are passed down with biology and behavior. Every time I fill out a familial health history, I am keenly aware of the reach of ACEs. Almost every adult on my maternal and paternal sides suffers from hypertension or high cholesterol. They take some kind of pill or pills daily. All three of my grandparents died from cancer. I never met Daddy's father. My dad was diagnosed with prostate cancer in August 2021. Several people in my family have suffered major and minor strokes, some more than one. Some people are diabetic. Several people have battled with alcoholism and drug abuse.

I refuse to believe these issues all stem from poor diet and lack of exercise. My grandmother was born in 1936. She told me stories of how her mom cleaned the homes of White people. Grandma told me Granddaddy had a rough upbringing. The amount of stress that the elders in my family endured was tremendous. Discrimination, poverty, and racism take their toll on more than a person's psyche.

Momma always talks about having never been a child because she was always raising kids, in the sense that she regularly cared for her siblings while Grandma and Grandaddy worked. Adult responsibilities being thrust upon a child is stressful. The science detailing the effects ACEs can have on a person's health is undisputed though not an absolute certainty. We can proactively work to prevent future occurrences of ACEs and heal from the past.

By the time you finish reading this book, I want this to be ingrained in your mind and your heart, "Young people should avoid abuse, not simply recover from it."

CHAPTER 2

BODY AUTONOMY

———

Growing up, pretty much every kid I knew was told, "Give Grandma, Auntie so and so—or insert any other adult relative or family friend—a hug or kiss." It was said in a loving, playful manner but was still a directive, nonetheless. Never mind that sometimes I didn't even know the person. It'd been that way since birth. I never questioned it. I don't even think the thought occurred to me that I could. When an adult told you to do something, you did it.

Body autonomy is the right for a person to govern what happens to their body without external influence or coercion. According to Dr. Shalon Nienow, child abuse pediatrician and medical clinical director at The Chadwick Center for Children and Families at Rady Children's and assistant clinical professor of pediatrics at University of California San Diego School of Medicine, "body autonomy is an important concept for all children to be taught and to understand. A child who knows they are in control of their body is less likely to fall victim to sexual abuse, sexual assault, and later intimate partner violence." (Nienow, 2019)

"They are also more likely to disclose any abusive events that should happen to them." (Nienow, 2019)

Child sexual abuse (CSA) is far more prevalent than most people realize. Studies show that about one in ten children will be sexually abused before their eighteenth birthday. Nearly 70 percent of all reported sexual assaults (including assaults on adults) occur to children aged seventeen and under. Youth have higher rates of sexual assault victimization than do adults. In 2000, the rate for youth aged twelve to seventeen was 2.3 times higher than for adults. And, of children who are sexually abused, 20 percent are abused before the age of eight.

I am in that 20 percent.

I don't remember anyone—not my mom, dad, grandmother, godmother, aunts, uncles, Sunday school teachers, doctors, or schoolteachers—teaching me about body autonomy.

No one taught me that during puberty, I would develop breasts, hips, a fuller bottom and that I would begin to feel and experience certain physiological changes.

No one told me that older boys, teens, young adult males, and men would also take notice of my developing breasts, hips, and fuller bottom.

No one told me that older boys, teens, young adult males, and men should not be attracted to girls.

No one told me these people should not have certain conversations with girls.

No one told me these people should not look at, touch, kiss, or rub girls, period.

What people did tell me was, "Don't get pregnant." *How do I make certain not to get pregnant if I don't even know how to get pregnant?* People also told me, "Don't be fast. Don't be mannish." *What's that even mean?* People told me in no uncertain terms, "What happens in this house stays in this house." To me, that meant that no one should be privy to the happenings inside the four walls of my home—not the drug abuse, the physical, emotional, and verbal abuse, not even the sexual abuse.

What's a kid to do? That's the million-dollar question because I had absolutely no clue. I didn't feel as though I had anyone to talk to.

Of course, the school had DARE, but they taught you that drugs were bad and not to do them. They didn't tell you who to call if your parent was abusing drugs. They made sure to tell us about the trouble we could get into, so why would I report my mom? Ma loved us. She was doing her best. *Who else would take care of us?*

Telling was not an option. So, I become a combustible vault. Not knowing that one day, all these secrets were going to break through my so-called impenetrable vault or that I'd unwittingly give the key to an undeserving person. Either way, I was unprepared for what was to come.

Who was supposed to prepare me? Who's responsible for my lack of knowledge? What if the very people who were supposed to teach me were never taught themselves, resulting in generational hurt? Well, I believe in generational healing. No adult ever explicitly taught me my body was my own; that I could tell a person, any person, that I didn't want to be touched. Because I was never given that liberty, I made sure my children were empowered and knew their bodies were their own.

Class is in session.

Teaching children about body autonomy at a young age will protect them throughout life. These lessons are meant for children of any gender. It will teach them to how to stand up for themselves. It will help them show respect for others and to know it's unacceptable to force others to do something they don't want to do. Body autonomy creates boundaries when your child interacts with others. Through body autonomy, your child will gain a sense of security and independence in making their own choices about their bodies.

I'm from Louisville, Kentucky. My husband Devin is from Miami, Florida. After graduating from college, we moved to Atlanta, Georgia, to begin our careers. We knew not living close to family and only seeing them a few times a year would create initial barriers to our children's, David and Parker's, connection to them. We were also resolute in our decision to allow them to form relationships with our family on their terms.

Some family members called Parker spoiled because, as a baby and toddler, she did not want to be held by them. Sometimes Parker would not even speak. I reminded our family that Parker is unfamiliar with them and is uncomfortable. We had to teach our family and friends that we don't make our kids hug, kiss, high five, fist bump, or engage in any other bodily contact if they don't want to. As foreign as the concept sounds, we ask permission to hug and kiss our children.

Early on, we introduced the concept of personal space and anatomical terms for body parts, including genitalia. I remember having a discussion with Momma one day, and she said, "Starr, you can't teach them that," in response to me saying I was teaching David and Parker penis and vagina.

To which I replied, "Ma, I can and will."

I have represented adults in superior court who, when asked to explain the details of their case, have replied, "He put his thing in me." *What's "a thing?"* Ever heard genitalia described as "pocketbook," "purse," "flower," "cookie," "ding a ling," "peter wacker," "wee wee," "johnson" or "pistol?"

Genitals are just another body part, like your nose or your elbow. We do not have to speak in code to describe those parts, so why must we speak in code to describe genitals? Genitals are functioning body parts that serve a purpose. When children know anatomical names for body parts and are encouraged to use those terms, they are more likely to speak up if something happens to their body they don't like or to disclose if something inappropriate takes place. Anatomical terms are unambiguous and understood by all should a child disclose abuse. (Nienow, 2019)

The American Academy of Pediatrics describes the genital exam as a standard of care in all well-child visits and a priority at one year and every age between six and twenty-one. It is considered another way for physicians to help normalize the conversation and can reinforce that genitals are not something of which to be ashamed.

Before doctor visits, we explain to David and Parker that the doctor will look at their bodies, including their genitalia. We assure them that it's to check their health and reinforce the fact that the doctor is only allowed to see their bodies with permission, and Mommy and Daddy will be with them the entire time. The notion of not telling children the truth has run its course.

Preventing CSA starts with adults. If a child can't tell a parent, caregiver, or guardian *no* as it relates to their bodies, we are effectively telling them that their body is not under their control and they must yield it to an adult if told to do so.

Sex Positive Families, LLC provides education and resources that help families raise sexually healthy children using a shame-free, comprehensive, and pleasure-positive approach. They have been featured in *Parents*, Scary Mommy, and *HuffPost,* among other publications. They offer the following insight. When we demand affection from children without regard to the child's experience, we send the message that their body is an object for others' pleasure over their own. We place them in an inequitable power dynamic that makes it challenging for them to identify and assert their boundaries.

Adults are not entitled to a child's body. If a child wishes to share affection, it should be their choice without negotiation or pressure. They suggest the following prompts as ways to honor body sovereignty by asking before affection is shared:

- "May I give you a hug or kiss?"

- "I'd like to hug you. Is that okay?"

- "Would you like to share a hug?"

Sex Positive Families adds, "If a child's response is not an affirmative and voluntary yes or agreement, it's a no." Don't respond with, "Aw, come on!" "Just one?" or, "You're making me sad!" That's coercion.

Teaching about body autonomy can seem so simple at times and be so hard at others. The practice of giving children power over their bodies, rather than ownership by their parents, has not always been the way in society. Children are human beings with fundamental rights. It is their absolute right to be safe.

In speaking with family and friends over the years, I've come to realize that adults are uncomfortable in their own skin. We must fight against the ideologies ingrained within us. For too long, many of us have internalized patriarchal ideologies about our bodies and felt subsequent shame. It's time to dismantle these oppressive narratives.

CHAPTER 3

THE BLEACHER REPORT

Masculine gender socialization confines men to *macho* boxes that deny their vulnerability or that they can be victims at all. Victims are associated with weakness and powerlessness, and men are socialized to seek and use power to their advantage. But boys and men are victims too. (Opening the Circle, 2021)

Historically, recognition of sexual abuse of boys and men, in addition to resources for them, has been limited. Though slowly, this is changing. Sexual abuse devastates the lives of countless male victims. As we understand the impact of sexual abuse and develop and create effective supports to help victims heal, boys and men, stories like Kevin's must be included.

I met Kevin and his wife while living in Atlanta. We both were working in the child sexual abuse (CSA), antitrafficking space. Kevin is an advocate, author, speaker, and founder of The Twelve Project. Kevin created The Twelve Project to be the bridge between the lack of knowledge and awareness about abuse and people's desire to learn. He provides resources with the aim of healing and teaching individuals, families, and communities. Kevin and I support one another's organizations. Kevin is a married, professional, God-fearing Black man. A pervasive and damaging myth is that boys and men can't be victims of sexual abuse and violence.

$$t + h = 3 \; \left(\tfrac{ab}{us}\right)3 \; \frac{a\sqrt{1g}+0}{r^{\shortmid} \pm th^{(n)}} \quad \textbf{KEVIN} \quad t + h = 3 \; \left(\tfrac{ab}{us}\right)3 \; \frac{a\sqrt{1g}+0}{r^{\shortmid} \pm th^{(n)}}$$

I looked different. Only twelve, I was small in stature, had a speech impediment, and was bullied at school. I wanted this old concrete weight set, but my mom couldn't afford it. A friend of mine had a set, so he let me use his. We talked about our lives as we lifted. I noticed he was always home alone. His mom battled with drug addiction. We became close.

Some considered my friend odd, but nobody messed with him. He had muscles. And I wanted some. Lifting weights every day after school became our thing. Mom gave me one rule. Get home before dark. The night of my sexual assault, I was heading home from my friend's house. We were talking. Time got away from me. It was dark. I panicked, thinking, *Mom's going to get me.*

Because I was late, I took the shortcut through Booker T. Washington High School. The stadium sat down in the ground and looked like a dome without a covering. As I was walking, a guy came up the stairs startling me. I stopped. I looked.

He said to me, "Hey, I stole some weights out of the gym, and if you help me get them, I'll give you some."

I was thinking, *Wait, this is what I want!* I said, "Okay," and followed him down the stairs. It never occurred to me that he could be lying. I mean, he stole them in the first place! All I was thinking was, *Let me get these weights.*

I followed him under the bleachers.

He lit a match. He said, "Get on your hands and knees and see if you see the weights."

I didn't see them. I thought he was mistaken about where he put them. He went deeper into the bleachers. I followed. It was darker. He told me to look again. I knew something was wrong when I didn't see weights the second time.

He started beating me. I was confused. I didn't know what he wanted. He pushed me down on my knees and put his hands around my neck. He pulled his penis out and said, "You gonna suck it, and you bet not bite it."

I'd never had sex. I'd never been introduced to sex. I did as I was told.

Once he was finished, he made me turn over, and he tried to insert his penis into my rectum. He couldn't get it in. He grew increasingly upset. He hit me in the small of my back as though it was my fault.

He continued to try to penetrate me and got it in a little bit, but by this time, I was making noise. He told me, "Shut the fuck up and take your pants off." I guess he thought with my pants off, he could fully get inside me. I thought, *If I take my pants off, I won't make it out of here alive.*

As I was pretending to take my pants off, I noticed he was taking his off too. When he bent down, I took off running. He ran after me but fell because his pants were around his ankles. I ran out of the darkness onto the football field toward the fence. I had to make it over. I looked back to see how far behind me he was. He had taken off his belt and was wrapping it around his hand. I ran faster. Faster.

I jumped the fence and ran into the street. Cars were driving by, but they couldn't see me because it was dark. I didn't care if I got hit or not. I just wanted to get away from him. Cars slammed on brakes, but nobody stopped. I looked back at him. He didn't jump the fence, though, probably because of the cars slowing down. I guess he figured it was time for him to keep going.

I was bloodied. No shoes. No shirt. People were staring, but they didn't say anything.

When I made it home, Mom asked what had happened? I told her I was robbed. I said, "The guys took my shirt and shoes, but I got away." Growing up on the south side of Memphis, that was believable. Mom wanted to call the police, but I told her not to. I felt like the police would have gotten the truth out of me. I never told anybody. I lived with it, hidden.

Ironically, a couple of years later, I graduated from junior high. My friend dropped out. I told him I wanted to play football. He said, "As small as you is, you crazy." I don't know what drove me to do it, but I went down to that same football stadium where I was assaulted and told the coach I was going to be his starting running back. Coach laughed. I made the team.

I played football, dressed out, and walked past the same set of bleachers and not once thought about my assault. It was like I was a different person.

The night of my assault, I had an out-of-body experience and never returned. Once I got away—alive—I started over. I left that little boy under those bleachers. I always tell people my assailant got away, but his accomplice followed me home, which was trauma. Growing up, I never made the connection. I love a quote I heard somebody say, "When a child is abused, a whole generation is affected." I think it's true.

I never had kids. I feared I wouldn't be a good father. I was addicted to sex. Sex was how I proved I wasn't gay, how I proved my value, my worth. It affected my ability to have meaningful relationships. I was so closed off. I never knew this one assault would affect me for the rest of my life.

I hid that experience my entire life. I didn't know it until God made me look back on it.

I played football. I left football and joined the military. I left the military to join the police force, becoming a special victims detective. I left the force to become a minister. I hid behind these uniforms, coverings that made people see outside of me while keeping them from getting close to me. This worked for a while, but I was losing control.

Prior to my marriage, I had sexual escapades. I drank. I needed help. My pastor asked me to see a therapist. I told him no, so Pastor had the therapist come to church. The title of the therapist's message was, "You're Not God." The message was about the healing process. Shortly after that message, I began therapy.

The first thing the therapist told me was, "You don't trust me because I'm a man." He never knew my story. He just picked up on it. I said, "No." He said, "How do I make you feel?" That was the first time anybody ever asked me that. He put a mirror in front of me and asked, "What do you see?"

I couldn't say one positive thing about myself. I wept the entire session. It was the first time I was listened to. He heard my pain without me telling my story.

From those sessions, I learned to listen to myself when I'm hurting. I now noticed that certain feelings would surface if I failed, felt rejected, or when things weren't going right. I was able to catch myself whereas before I couldn't. Now I'd think, *What's the alternative to destructive behavior?*

Before I began my healing process, I would feel rejected if my wife didn't want to have sex. I would immediately think, *Oh, what's wrong with me?* When really, she just wasn't in the mood. When thoughts of wanting a drink, watching porn, or infidelity would rise, I used to deny having the thoughts. Now, I hear myself.

Being heard is the pathway to healing.

Learning about trauma is also part of my healing process.

It's important for me to know not only about the event or abuse but how it affects the brain. Trauma is not abnormal. Trauma is a normal response to an abnormal event.

My mom is an abuse victim too. She says that before I was born, she was walking to the bus when a guy picked her up and put her in the trunk. She started kicking out of the trunk and escaped. All these years later, I wonder if Mom did what I did? I wonder if more happened to her? Did she get away and never talk about it?

I never knew my father. Mom told me he was murdered when I was born. My uncle would say, "Yeah, he was murdered. What's your dad's name? You don't even know."

I told him, "My dad's name was John." My uncle replied, "Sure… his name was John."

My oldest brother's father was a pimp. The rumor was he trafficked Mom, and I was the result of rape. Mom never confirmed it, but based on the stories my family shared, I think it's true. Between my mom having dated a pimp, her near kidnapping, and family gossip, it's not hard to believe.

Abuse has not only become a part of our lives. It's become a way of our lives.

Families have become anesthetized.

When I train detectives, I tell them families are not going to readily share with you because of the adage, "What happens in this house stays in this house." People are trying to survive in their environments. To some that means, don't talk to the police. Don't say what you see. It'll go away.

One of the most disturbing cases I worked as a special victims detective was when a young lady came to me feeling suicidal.

She'd gone to a family reunion and saw the uncle who had abused her. She was going to kill him. She had a gun. She talked to me first. She said, "Nobody believes me. My family knows this man did this to me."

When I spoke to her mother, she said, "Detective, why don't you just get over that? That happened years ago. Everybody knows that happened, and we've moved on with our lives. We're all having a good time at the family reunion. She shows up and starts a fight with him. That's the past." I was blown away. Everybody knew.

I called the district attorney's office. The statute of limitations had run. Her uncle could no longer be prosecuted. I was scared to tell her. I had to tell her in person. I walked into the lobby and walked right past her. I didn't recognize her. I confirmed with my secretary I had a two o'clock appointment.

She spoke up, "It's me, Detective." She had transformed. She followed me into my office.

I said, "I've got some bad news. The district attorney can't prosecute the case." She said, "That's okay. I found somebody who believed me. I'm fine."

I was shocked. She walked out of my office a different person. I'll never forget sitting at my desk thinking, *Wow*. The first day she came to see me, she was torn up. Her hair was a mess. When she came in the second time, I saw a stark contrast—all from being heard. Believed.

I bought a book called *Crime Victims Speak* because I wanted to hear what other victims had to say about their encounters with law enforcement. A lot of those victims said they had a worse encounter with law enforcement than they did with the actual perpetrator. Victims said the response to their outcry made them feel worse. That's the reason I left law enforcement. When I tried to change the culture of our response to abuse victims, I was told, "Get back to your cubicle. We pay you to lock people up." I resigned.

Do you know how much courage it takes for a child to disclose abuse? I tell families, "Your response to a child's outcry is important. Your child could resent you for the rest of their life if they know you know they are being abused and you do nothing." Families have to build cultures and environments where it's safe for children to have these conversations. Educate yourself on what's happening in your environment. Give children space and opportunity to tell you anything. Your response not only affects this child. It also affects their children.

One of my biggest pushes is to educate families. I was speaking around the world at conferences, colleges, and schools when I decided this wasn't just a conversation for courtrooms and classrooms. We need to be in living rooms too. That's why I created The Twelve Project, to be the bridge between the lack of knowledge and awareness about abuse and people's desire to learn. We provide resources with the aim of healing and teaching individuals, families, and communities. But here's the caveat, nobody wants to have the conversation.

Some of my biggest pushback comes from the Black community. I tell them we use the same methodology the slave master used to control the slaves on our children. We have to get to a place where we are able to have these conversations. CSA affects every area of our lives. We have made women objects. We no longer respect the mothers of our children or the ones who birth us. Those mothers grew up not knowing fully how to nurture a child. Yes, they provide housing and food, but a child needs nurturing. If we want to stop the violence in our communities, we've got to stop the silence in our communities.

This may sound extreme, but abuse is the root cause of everything bad in our culture. We deal with the symptoms. We deal with violence, addiction, racism, and sexism, but at the core of all those issues, abuse is the culprit. If we educate ourselves about abuse at the family level, we can stop it at a greater level. It starts with education.

One day I received a call at the office. At the time, I was the only detective there. I answered. It was the district attorney's office. An attorney had double-booked herself to speak to some nurses about sexual assault, and she was looking for a speaker. They were in a bind. They asked if I would go. I agreed, thinking, *I don't know what to say, so I'll just tell my story.* I was more nervous about standing in front of people than I was to tell my story.

I told my story. Everyone in the audience was crying. People started coming up to me, saying, "I was abused too," or, "This is my first time telling anybody." They asked me to speak again. They asked if I would be willing to travel out of state. I was. They told me they couldn't pay me because no one knew who I was. I still accepted. It was a child abuse conference in North Carolina. I'd literally just spent my last money on a $1,500 car. It was leaking oil and fluids from everywhere. I had a pocket full of change I was saving up for food. I was broke. How I was going to make it to North Carolina? I said, "Okay, God, I'll drive."

The first day I spoke, people cried again. On the break, I bought food from the Bojangles across the street using my pocket change. I figured I would snack on a five-piece for the duration of the three-day conference. On the second day of the conference, I went back to the room I spoke in the day before, and a huge crowd waited outside the room. I thought, *They must have moved me. They've put me in a smaller room. A big speaker's in there now.*

I was standing in line waiting to talk to someone to see where I needed to go, and a lady walked up to me and said, "Oh, you're here."

I said, "Yeah, did they move me?"

She said, "No, sweetie, you're the talk of the conference. Everybody is trying to get in your class."

After speaking that time, everything took off.

Yours in Safety, Kevin

It resonated to my core when Kevin said, "The night of my assault, I had an out-of-body experience and never returned. I left that little boy under the bleachers." I'm sure we can all relate to experiencing something we'd rather forget. Kevin isn't alone. My abuse spanned a five-year period, and I've suppressed a good bit of it.

Dissociation is a psychological process that often occurs in response to extreme trauma or pain—an automatic response determined by severity of the trauma and the individual's ability to endure psychological pain and emotional distress. Dissociation is a disruption in normal information processing and allows the person to block negative emotions and experiences from consciousness and compartmentalize traumatic memories. Abuse victims dissociate to escape the abuse. They create a distance between what is happening to their bodies and the feelings and thoughts that are connected to the experience. Many sexual abuse victims report gaps in memory, varying from events to chunks of lost childhood memories in which they cannot retrieve memories. (MOSAC, 2021)

Have you ever just wanted to forget?

As a result of his abuse, Kevin battled with suicidal ideation, as many survivors do. He's not alone in his struggle. Joel Leon penned an essay titled "For Black Boys Considering Suicide," in which he shares his experience of sexual abuse at five years old and the dreaded aftermath. Joel says:

"As boys, we never spoke about these things, especially Black boys. The boys become men, who may eventually raise other boys, quiet boys, too afraid to break their silence."

Collectively, our silence is deafening, especially in the Black community. For most men, the mere idea of being a victim of sexual abuse or assault is hard to reconcile. Men and boys need to be heard. They are no less of a man. Their sexual orientation is not up for debate. The outrage you feel when women and girls are abused and assaulted, keep the same energy for men and boys.

CHAPTER 4

BRUTE FORCE

It's been said that behind every strong person is a story that gave them no choice. I'm not sure it applies in every context, but it definitely does in the survivor realm. The relatability of shared trauma with others has served me well in my healing journey. Nimi and I met on a SurvivorRevive panel about grooming. You'll learn more about SurvivorRevive later in the book. After the panel, SurvivorRevive's founder Kelley, Nimi, and I continued our own discussion.

According to Darkness to Light, child grooming is a deliberate process by which offenders gradually initiate and maintain sexual relationships with victims in secrecy. Think of it as offenders lying in wait. They slowly overcome natural boundaries long before sexual abuse occurs. The three of us shared instances of how our abusers groomed us, our parents, caregivers, and community.

Grooming can occur in stages. It typically starts with the abuser targeting a child's perceived vulnerability. They'll gain the trust of the child and the child's caregiver(s) to gain access to the child. Once trust is established, the abuser will start fulfilling the child's need(s). It could be something tangible like gifts and money or more attention and affection. Isolation happens next. The abuser creates situations in which they are alone with the child to reinforce their relationship by cultivating a sense that they love and understand the child in a way others do not. Once emotional dependence and trust have been built, the perpetrator progressively sexualizes the relationship. The progression can take form by talking, with pictures, or creating situations in which both are naked. The abuser exploits the child's natural curiosity and trust using stimulation to advance the sexual nature of the relationship. Once sexual abuse occurs, abusers commonly use secrecy, blame, and threats to maintain the child's participation and continued silence. Abusers use emotional manipulation as a means of control. The child may also feel that the loss of the relationship, or the consequences of exposing it, will be more damaging and humiliating than continuing the unhealthy relationship. (Darkness to Light, 2021)

The key to understanding grooming is that it is very hard to detect when it is happening as many of the grooming behaviors in and of themselves appear completely innocuous, and in many cases, they are. It is estimated that about half of those who abuse children use grooming behaviors. Research shows that people are generally quite poor at identifying grooming behaviors before it is revealed that abuse has occurred. Only in hindsight do the behaviors appear suspicious. (Jeglic, 2019)

This is why it is especially important to know who is around your children and be aware of how they are interacting with them. While this may result in you being an overly suspicious parent, it is always better to be safe than sorry. Many child-serving organizations that have had sex scandals involving grooming, like the Catholic Church and Boy Scouts, have now developed policies where children are not allowed to be alone with adults. (Jeglic, 2019)

$$t + h = 3 \ \left(\tfrac{ab}{us}\right)3 \ \ \frac{a \sqrt{1g} + 0}{r^{\iota} \pm th^{(n)}} \quad \textbf{NIMI} \quad t + h = 3 \ \left(\tfrac{ab}{us}\right)3 \ \ \frac{a \sqrt{1g} + 0}{r^{\iota} \pm th^{(n)}}$$

I saw my abusers once or twice a week. It was three of them, brothers. The sons of family friends. I was groomed. They used threats and violence to make me participate. Thankfully, our families stopped talking for other reasons. That's when the abuse stopped.

The oldest brother was either nineteen or twenty. The middle brother was probably a year or two younger than him, and the youngest was sixteen or seventeen. I was three. The abuse ended when I was seven. They would be with me together and individually. The oldest brother started it. The middle brother was by far the worst. He was evil.

My abusers are probably retired or approaching retirement now. They got married. Had kids. My fear was always that they were going to do this to someone else. I disclosed the abuse to my school counselor at fifteen. She told my parents. I started therapy right away.

My parents believed me. A lot of survivors aren't believed, or they're made to feel like they took part in it, so they are in some way at fault. I've worked with many survivors, and it's heartbreaking to know how many aren't believed.

The abuse impacted me in ways no one else is going to know that this is where—said behavior—is stemming from, but I know. Because of my experience, I earned a degree in psychology. I've done a lot of work and spent a significant portion of my life in therapy.

I had to learn to trust, to set boundaries, to form attachments. I have control issues over my environment. Even still in small ways, like making sure the cups in my cabinet are all aligned. It's important that my environment is controlled.

Funny enough, I have four girlfriends, all therapists. One asked me, "What if the cups aren't turned the right way, or what if everything's not in its place?"

I looked at her and said, "The world's not going to be a happy place!"

To which she says, "In the grand scheme of things..."

I interject, "You don't think I know that in the grand scheme of things, it don't matter?"

It matters. If I don't have control over my environment, I fear losing control over everything else. I understand that. I know what it is. I don't need someone to tell me that. Am I ever going to be able to work past that? I have no fucking clue. Honestly, at this point, I actually don't care. It works for me. My mom and dad get it and they don't. Sometimes it drives me nuts. It's unnerving at times. It impedes my life and interaction with others. I am a little better than I was a couple of years ago. But I live alone. And so, guess what,

I'm the only one who puts my stuff away, so it's always in the right place.

Because of the physical stress my body has endured, I can no longer handle any form of stress. I stopped doing the work I was doing because of my body's physical response and reaction to the stress of it. My body can't seem to handle it. I've had high blood pressure since I was in grade five. I only know this because I used to get allergy shots, and the doctor would take my blood pressure and ask me, "Why is your blood pressure so high?"

I'd respond, "I don't know. I don't even know what blood pressure is."

I've done different things at different times during my healing journey. I started therapy at fifteen and continued until nineteen. I stopped until I was about twenty-three. I went back to therapy until I was about twenty-eight or twenty-nine. And then, a few years later, I was in therapy again for about a year or two. I'm a firm believer that "You can only help someone as much as you are helped or as healthy as you are." I can't help someone rise above my own health. For that reason, when I worked with women and children, it was important I remained grounded and aware of my own triggers.

I'm self-aware. I analyze why I do the things I do and why others do the things they do. I'm aware of my own behavior and reactions, whether they're positive or negative. I try to keep my emotions in check. I don't always do a good job of it. As a child, right from the beginning, I wondered, why would they do this to me? Why would one human do this to another? This is the only reason I went into psychology. Otherwise, trust me, I would not have. I wanted to know what makes one person do something. Whether it's, "Why does one person respond this way?" "Why does one person react this way?" "Why did you behave the way that you did?" I was looking for an answer, for a reason. Not that I found one, but it enabled me to take stock of my own behavior.

To be honest, working out is probably one of the best things for me. It's four or five days for me, at minimum four, max six. I'm not going to do seven. Regardless of what I'm going through, it makes me feel so much better.

I also have a great network of people. I believe the reason I may have somewhat succeeded in putting my past in the past is because of my support network. Whether one person or five, it was vital for me to have someone in my corner—my parents, my siblings, my friends. Even now, I'm close with about twelve or thirteen women and three to four men. We share mutual respect. Those relationships over the course of time have kept me grounded and allowed me to see where I've been, where I come from, and where I am.

I share my story for others to be aware that this happens right under your nose, more often than you'd like to believe. If you're a survivor, don't feel like you have to be silent. I started the hashtag #notmysecret so survivors could use their names without shame. Some circumstances warrant a name change. But when I was in grade eight or grade nine, realizing I had been abused, I would read all these books. I was going to counseling, and they were telling me it was not my fault. But when I read these books, the names were always changed, or their identifying factors had been altered. I thought, *If it's not my fault, why are they changing their names?* The "not my secret" hashtag is an awareness movement to empower survivors that it's not our secret to keep. We didn't do anything wrong.

For nonsurvivors, watch your language, watch your reactions, and watch what you say to people. If you don't know what to say, shut the fuck up. Just stay silent. Don't have a physical or verbal reaction to what you've just been told. If you can't say anything else, can you just say, "I'm sorry?" Your sorry doesn't mean anything to the person, but at least you're not messing them up with your reaction. I've had people whose eyes have popped out at me or reacted with visible nervousness. It didn't happen to you, or maybe it did. If it did, I'm sorry I'm triggering something in you that makes you respond in this way, but this isn't about you. This is about me saying something to you.

I understand that not everyone has the capacity to control their response, and I'm working on not being impacted by someone else's reaction. It's a lot of work being a survivor. You have to go deep not to respond or react to every negatively responding person because you've already experienced so many things on a negative level. Can you not make us do some more work?

Yours in Safety, Nimi

I agree with Nimi 1,000 percent. Being a survivor is work. It is work to endure the abuse, to move past it, to relive it, to work through it, to advocate for others. Most times, we feel so alone. We suffer in silence. For victims of CSA, it is remarkable to disclose abuse at all, regardless of their age. Data from the Department of Justice suggests that 86 percent of CSA goes unreported altogether. However, when victims of CSA do report, a high percentage of them delay disclosure well into adulthood. (Child USA, 2020)

The delay in disclosing CSA happens for a variety of complex and overlapping reasons. Child victims face many barriers that prevent disclosure. Among other barriers, children often:

1. lack the knowledge needed to recognize sexual abuse,

2. lack the ability to articulate that they've been abused,

3. don't have an adult they can disclose their abuse to,

4. don't have opportunities to disclose abuse,

5. aren't believed when they try to disclose.

Trauma that results from the abuse, power differentials between the child victim and adult perpetrator, and institutional power dynamics all impact the delay. (Child USA, 2020)

It is critical to understand the science behind delayed disclosure because it influences society's perception of CSA survivors. After disclosing that they were abused, survivors often face an array of questions casting doubt on their allegation. Many of these questions hinge on the fact that the survivor did not disclose the abuse as a child. Without an understanding of the evidence-based pattern of delayed disclosure, it is difficult for individuals—whether they are loved ones, legal authorities, lawmakers, etc.—to comprehend why victims would wait years before telling their story. (Child USA, 2020)

Fortunately for Nimi and me, we were believed when we disclosed our abuse. That is not always the case. I don't know how it would have impacted me had Kia not believed me when I disclosed it to her. Her belief in me gave me hope. Her support meant everything to me. Imagine how different my experience would have been had either of us been equipped with the knowledge to recognize, disclose, and report abuse. Most adults are ill-equipped too. Plausible deniability is self-serving. Abuse victims deserve better.

CHAPTER 5

ARTIFICIAL INTELLIGENCE

Have you ever spoken to someone and your lives were so uniquely parallel that it was almost as if they were telling your story? That was my experience when Nancy shared her truth with me. Over a two-week period, she was groomed and then molested by her older cousin. According to Defend Innocence, a public charity with a mission to eradicate child sexual abuse and its effects, the term child-on-child sexual abuse (COCSA) is defined as *sexual activity between children that occurs without consent, without equality (mentally, physically, or in age), or as a result of physical or emotional coercion.* What this means is that a power differential exists between the two children, whether that is in age, size, or ability.

Growing up, I'd hear people say so and so were kissing cousins. As a child, I never gave it much thought. I've since learned its original meaning—which dates back to at least the mid-1800s in Virginia—meant a family member one knows well enough to give a kiss upon greeting. (Leftly, 2021) Somewhere along the way, the term morphed into casual acceptance of exploratory sexual behaviors between kids, related or not. It wasn't okay then. It's not okay now.

$$t + h = 3 \ \left(\tfrac{ab}{us}\right)3 \ \frac{a\sqrt{1g}+0}{r^i \pm th^{(n)}}$$ **NANCY** $$t + h = 3 \ \left(\tfrac{ab}{us}\right)3 \ \frac{a\sqrt{1g}+0}{r^i \pm th^{(n)}}$$

Some ten-year-olds do not have the opportunity to travel out of the country to visit family during the summer for two weeks, but I did. My trip was memorable too, but not for the reasons you would think. Allow me to unpack an unforgettable vacation.

My sixteen-year-old male cousin invited me into his room and pulled a magazine out of a drawer. "Nancy, I want to show you something," he said. He opened the magazine with images of children partially and fully nude. I didn't know what it was. I was confused. "Have you ever seen this before?"

"No."

"Well, don't tell anyone."

"Okay."

He may have shown me the magazine one or two more times that first week.

One day, while taking a shower, my cousin climbed up to the lower part of the roof and looked in on me through the window. Noticing him, I quickly closed the window curtain. That would not be our last encounter. The night before we left, he decided to do more than just look. That night, my mom, uncle, and aunt went out, leaving me, my little brother, and his little brother in my cousin's care. That was the night he molested me. He had groomed me for that moment.

The flight back to America and the safe distance it gave me from him saved me. He whispered in my ear before we left to board the plane that he looked forward to seeing me again. I am certain had I remained in his proximity, the abuse would have continued, considering how his advances increased over the two-week period. Fortunately, I never saw him again until many years later. By then, I was an adult.

For me, age ten was difficult emotionally and physically. I was prepubescent. My body hadn't yet transformed, but I was experiencing sensations I could not explain. I was confused. After the abuse, I was particularly uncomfortable around older boys and men. I did not want to show my body. I struggled with why this happened and wondered what I did to deserve this. At that time, I was drawn toward sexually explicit books and writings.

While I was able to physically escape my abuser, I was emotionally scarred. There was no escaping the shame. I would carry the baggage for many years. I didn't share my experience with my mom until my late forties. She was shocked and deeply hurt. She felt badly because she had no idea. Growing up, we didn't have conversations about personal boundaries, relationships with others, or sex.

Around the same time as my abuse, I found out that my dad was not my biological father. This was disclosed to me only after I returned home from a visit to the local courthouse with my parents. At that time, the judge approved his legal adoption of me. Talk about a double whammy. I was devastated and confused. The combination of these two traumatic situations was a crushing blow.

I wasn't very trusting. As I matured, I became sexually promiscuous. I was more comfortable connecting with men physically rather than emotionally. I was particularly drawn to emotionally unavailable men. Because of my fear of abandonment, it was difficult for me to be in a relationship with a man. It took years of therapy for me to work through my self-destructive behavior and the cycle attached to it.

My journey to healing has had its peaks and valleys. I realized that in threatening situations, I would at times revert back to that little ten-year-old girl. I needed to address her pain. It's taken decades to heal that scarring. The next time I saw my abuser, I was twenty-seven years old. It was very awkward. We were at my uncle's funeral. He apologized for what he did to me, and I accepted his apology. That was the last time I saw him. We remain safely separated. I realize not all women who suffer abuse are as fortunate. Seeing my abuser caused me to relive the experience.

God works in wonderful and mysterious ways. I met my biological father, got married, and was blessed with two beautiful daughters. From a young age, I talked to them about setting boundaries, not allowing people to touch their bodies, and encouraging them to talk to me about anything. I'm most proud that they are fifteen and eighteen, and when I asked if anybody ever touched them inappropriately, they said no. As they were growing up, I was vigilant about who was around them and put male family members on notice that "If anyone touches or hurts my girls, I'm coming after them." I'm thankful my girls never experienced what I did.

I've always said, "People act the way they do for a reason." You'll hear people sometimes comment, "Oh, that girl is a hoe." Instead of judging her, pause to envision what may have led her to behave that way. When a person is objectified, abandoned, or degraded by people who are supposed to protect them, it destabilizes them. At times there's a tendency for them to feel and act as if they are unworthy of love and respect.

I want people to know it's not strangers they need to be afraid of. It's the people (family and friends) who have access to their children. It's their inner circle. Predators are unassuming. The people you least expect to be predators are normally the predators. That's why we call them "the predator within."

We need to let children know it's okay to talk about sensitive issues and their bodies at a young age. Give them the proper vocabulary they will need and model the behavior to stand up to people when put in uncomfortable or inappropriate situations. Teach children that if an adult or young person tells them to keep a secret relating to their body, they should share that secret right away. Children are not secret keepers.

For those who have never experienced abuse, show compassion. People don't ask to be victimized, and its impact manifests in different ways. Try to understand and not judge.

Unfortunately, my experience is not unique. I've learned not to allow it to define me. If I can use my experience to help others, it's worth it.

Yours in Safety, Nancy

Some may argue there is a slippery slope with grooming, a hierarchy of sorts. When I think about my own experiences, I don't believe I was groomed. My abuse happened one day without warning. Then it became routine. Not knowing whether my cousins ever discussed their interactions with me, one could say my first cousin groomed me for the others.

According to Defend Innocence, one-third of all victimization occurs between people who are both under the age of eighteen. In situations of COCSA, both children need help. The child being abused needs the appropriate care to mitigate the lifelong trauma and symptoms many survivors of CSA experience. The child initiating the harmful sexual behavior may need to see a medical/mental health professional to help them work through these age-inappropriate sexual behaviors. I'd be lying if I didn't acknowledge the fact I sometimes wonder what happened to my cousins. Who hurt them? Who mistreated them? Who directly or indirectly exposed them to mature material? It's heartbreaking.

FIVE FACTS ABOUT COCSA:
Ages twelve to fourteen are the peak ages for an adolescent to engage in harmful sexual behaviors.

During this age range, puberty begins. Kids experience a lot of changes. Depending on their view of sex, they may target someone younger, smaller, or with cognitive or physical limitations.

Seventy percent of all adult perpetrators have between one and nine victims.

When a child or teen victimizes another child, they need help immediately to prevent the victimization of others.

As many as 40 percent of children who are sexually abused are victimized by older or more powerful children.

It's equally as important to find ways to protect your child from sexual abuse as it is to protect them from perpetrating abuse against others.

Sex offenses are the crimes least likely to involve strangers as perpetrators.

Reporting it is the best thing you can do for *both* children involved.

Children who disclose their abuse within one month are at a reduced risk for depression.

If your child can talk about the abuse with you, they are less likely to suffer from depression later in life because of it. Believe them when they talk to you or disclose to you. One of the most important things you can do is *listen.*

Since publicly sharing my story, several people have shared with me that their family members abused them. To find out a family member is abusing a loved one is stressful. You may even be tempted to keep the abuse a secret or pick a side.

Don't.

Let's not disregard harmful behavior as "kids being kids." (Defend Innocence, 2021)

It's reckless.

Let's not disregard the abusive nature of anyone.

CHAPTER 6

PEER REVIEW

It's frustrating when anyone—physicians, scholars, or my personal favorite, experts—label our experiences. We are the experts of our experience. A certain assurance comes with meeting and getting to know other survivors on our healing journeys. It's hard work, standing in solidarity, sharing our stories, and bit by bit, reclaiming what was stolen from us.

Each abuse victim is different, even in how they classify themselves, for instance, as a victim, survivor, thriver, overcomer, or something else altogether. Some abuse victims are free-flowing with the details of their story. Some are not. And while we're at it, let's address the word "story," too. Some people are of the mindset that when abuse victims refer to their experience as their "story," it somehow implies it's fictitious or embellished. It's not.

Citra and I met on the SurvivorRevive panel, Building Self-Worth, Self-Esteem. After the panel, she beat me to the punch, sending me a DM on Instagram asking if I would be a guest on her podcast. I literally was going to message her the same

day asking if I could interview her for *The Abuse Algorithm*.
Great minds think alike.

Citra is an author, activist, and founder of *Tis The Lyfe*, an
inclusive space for volunteers to learn and share their knowledge and skills, their stories, speak out, stand up and become
empowered to act upon injustice and inequality. A champion
of many causes, Citra is the codirector of *Hollaback Jakarta*,
a movement to end street harassment. She is also the host
of *Pleasure Girls Podcast* where she navigates the process of
maturity through womanhood while cultivating the space
for healing and growth by questioning biases, stereotypes,
and discrimination. Citra, having come into her own, is a
force to be reckoned with.

$$t + h = 3 \left(\tfrac{ab}{us}\right)3 \ \frac{a\sqrt{1g} + 0}{r^i \pm th^{(n)}}$$ **CITRA** $$t + h = 3 \left(\tfrac{ab}{us}\right)3 \ \frac{a\sqrt{1g} + 0}{r^i \pm th^{(n)}}$$

I was born in Jakarta, Indonesia. My dad is a diplomat, so
we moved around a lot. Dad was on duty in Ukraine for five
years. When we returned home, my Indonesian was not as
strong. I enrolled in a stepping stone school, the only one to
admit students midyear. Before then, I never had to immerse
myself in my own culture. I'd grown accustomed to international schools and the varying social and cultural differences.
It was totally different in Indonesian schools.

The semester had already begun. It was middle school, and
we were starting puberty. My first encounter with abuse was
at fourteen. He was a schoolmate. It happened on and off
for five years. He introduced me to what I thought *everyone
was doing*. I didn't want to be *the new girl* and *that girl* who

didn't understand her own language. They labeled me as a rich girl. I wasn't rich. I never represented myself as though I were. Because my family had lived around the world, they saw a status gap. It was intense. Girls kept their distance from me. Boys hung around me. I thought it was because I was a tomboy. I was more one of them. I played soccer. I was a jock. Then I realized that some of them liked me. I'd think *he's cute. He's handsome.* But I never got physical.

He told me, "All teens here do this." He taught me how to make out. How to kiss. He introduced me to my own body. It was a side of me I had never explored before. Sadly, I entered the world of sexuality through him. He was my boyfriend turned partner turned something weird.

Even though I'm fully immersed in the world of sexual violence now, when I think of grooming, I think of an adult with a child with the adult teaching the child. But this fourteen-year-old child groomed me emotionally. He made me feel things I'd never felt before. Once I educated myself with the tools and resources, I was able to label what he did to me.

He masturbated in front of me with our friends in the next room. He made me do things I would never do. Most of what he did to me was in my own home because he lived in my neighborhood. He'd wait and watch for my parents to leave home to come over.

Leaving Indonesia was my escape plan. I got away from him by running away to college in the States. I left my problems and my past. Later, I would have to confront it all. I had to face it.

While at university in the States, I was harassed. We'd gone to a frat party as a group. One guy kept trying to separate me from the group. By the end of the night, he managed to isolate me. He took my phone and went outside. I felt helpless the moment he took my phone away, like I had no lifelines. There was no light. It was dark, damp, and rainy.

He was shouting at me. He repeatedly pushed my head down to his private area for me to do things to him. He took his pants off and continued to shout. At that moment, I realized that in the States, garages had motion sensor lights. We were in front of a lot of houses with motion sensors. Not one person from inside the homes heard me or came outside if they did. We were shouting.

Something clicked inside of me. I couldn't process what was happening fast enough. When violence or harassment occurs suddenly, we don't really think, and that's why sometimes our reaction is not based on who we are. I pushed him. I kicked him. I screamed. I yelled, realizing those were all the things I wanted to do with my first abuser.

Thankfully, a shuttle bus was dropping off and picking up kids from the frat house. Once I saw the bus, I screamed. Luckily, someone I knew happened to be getting off the bus and saw me. At the same time, my friends came running out of the house like, "Oh my God, there you are!"

They rescued me. My male friends from the basketball team helped the most. Just know the guy ran off with his pants around his ankles. The entire basketball team, my friends, and I got on the shuttle bus.

I was crying. My friends didn't leave me. We all slept in the lobby of the dorm. One friend shared how the same thing happened to her. She questioned why she didn't scream out. I shared a lot of stories that night. Here I was, the only foreigner, international student surrounded by American students, and they treated me as though I was their own. Like I was their little sister or friend they'd known for years, only they hadn't. This was freshman year. We hadn't known one another that long. I was grateful.

Because I was an international student, I was assigned a guidance counselor. The next morning, we all went to see him. My friends waited in the lobby as I spoke with my counselor. He immediately sent me to the dean. The dean told the board of staff, who promptly checked the guy's record. Unsurprisingly, he was problematic. His offense toward me was the last straw. He was kicked out of the university.

That night was a turning point for me. I thought, *Wow. I spoke up. I defended myself. I got this. What would have happened if I had done this sooner or for others?* The puzzle pieces kept coming together after that, and I had to confront my past. Reflecting on my journey, my story, I think I initially disclosed to myself. I sat in a room. Alone. I talked it through. I recognized there'd been this disconnect from my body.

Then I told the people I trusted. They believed me. It reminded me of the time when I told my family I was uncomfortable around my first abuser. I was either fourteen or fifteen years old. I think because I was raised to be a strong archetype warrior, my family didn't take my outcry seriously.

When I told them something uncomfortable happened to me, they were like, "You're strong. Just kick him. You're not that weak." I bottled it inside. It hurt not to be believed. And in talking with survivors now, I've noticed a recurring theme of familial or parental disbelief.

From my experience with my first abuser, I became highly addicted to porn throughout middle and high school. He used porn as tutorials as to how he and I should engage. I developed mistrust and dislike for the boys and men around me.

I was lonely.

I didn't have meaningful relationships with girls. I was bullied. The abuse prevented me from relating with men and boys. I decided I would just use them and be done with it.

After the college incident, I reevaluated how I valued myself as a woman. My definition of a woman was misconstrued with society's perspective. I began a journey of getting to know me, my body included. I redefined my womanhood, my femininity. I no longer escaped difficult situations through masculine energy. There was a time when I loved when people would say, "Oh, you're just one of the boys." I internalized that thought process, which resulted in my reluctance to have women friends. Once I regained my own voice, I gained so much respect for the women around me and believed in sisterhood.

Years later, I moved back to Indonesia. I saw my first abuser again. He wasn't the same person. He wasn't the powerful jerk from middle and high school. I was different too. I viewed him differently. I didn't wish ill on him. He was raised under the same patriarchal religious influences as me. Older men around him talked about women in this way and easily disregarded them. It's still happening.

Sometimes we want revenge on our abusers. It's valid because we loathe them. I've grown into someone who can see my abuser as vulnerable and misguided. He was so wrong on what a man should be, what masculinity is, what he thinks the world is. He was fourteen too. My current partner and I believe he may have been an abuse victim too. Be clear, I'm not making excuses for him because even if he was abused, it doesn't justify what he did to me. For my own well-being, I've come to terms with this aspect of my experience for me to thrive.

Another huge turning point on my journey to healing was when I met my partner. This year marks our sixth year together. He's Indonesian and I never thought I would trust another Indonesian man again. Prior to my partner, I used men and spat them out of my life. This one had feelings. I saw his vulnerability. I thought, *Oh my God, boys can do that. Boys can cry. You're afraid of losing me?*

From day one, he was different. How we met. How he introduced himself. He was on a journey to becoming too. He learned a lot from me, and I learned more from him through his vulnerability and his ability to be present.

The media plays a role in how society defines CSA, especially when celebrities highlight their experiences of abuse. People should know that when it comes to abuse victims, it doesn't matter what your status or race is. An abuser could be famous, your neighbor, or a family member. Don't label abuse as one thing.

Listen to your children. Don't dismiss them.

Yours in Safety, Citra

Sexual abuse is fluid. There is no one-size-fits-all occurrence. No two situations are exactly alike. You can't check a box of predetermined experiences. Experiencing sexual abuse is miserable. Having to process it is worse.

At the start of your healing journey, it can be a bit of a repeated gut check as you relive it again and again. Very few adults recognize that children and adolescents also can present a risk to other children.

Stop It Now, an organization founded by child sexual abuse survivor, Fran Henry, reports that over a third of all sexual abuse of children is committed by someone under the age of eighteen. This can be a difficult issue to address, partly because it is often challenging for adults to think of the children or adolescents we know as capable of sexually abusing others. Also, it is not always easy to tell the difference between natural sexual curiosity and potentially abusive behaviors. Children, particularly younger children, may engage in inappropriate interactions without understanding the hurtful impact it has on others. For this reason, it may be more helpful to talk about a child's sexually "harmful" behavior rather than sexually "abusive" behavior. It is essential that all adults have the information needed to recognize potentially harmful activities at an early stage and seek help so the behaviors can be stopped.

As Citra shared her experiences with me, I thought about the Black, Brown, and White youth I've worked with over the years. I recalled how they were treated by their families, the juvenile justice systems, school administration, and other service providers when they disclosed. How people questioned their motives or explained away the situation. Cultural norms affect disclosure and reporting and are variously influenced by religion and global cultural trends. Reporting practices are influenced by sensitivity, fear, taboo, attitude, acceptable practices, and prejudice; also, community passivity, legal system inadequacies and weaknesses, and the general perceptions and attitudes toward sexual offenses against children contribute to a much-muted response to CSA.

Understanding the concept of CSA continues to be a challenge in many cultures. In a review of a population-based study from nineteen countries, only about half of victims had disclosed their abuse to anyone. The role and attitude of family and community continue to be cited as important factors in sexual abuse reporting, as well as the relationship between perpetrator and victim. It is argued that the interactions between children and parents are often driven by customary practices and personal beliefs, which may be in conflict with current thinking. The orientation toward collectivity makes disclosure very difficult and may explain why children in traditional households do not talk about sexual matters and are reluctant to report or support victims to avoid shame and possible repercussions of disclosure. (Shafe and Hutchinson, 2014)

You may not fully comprehend the gravity of you believing a child. Counseling is one part of the healing process. Being believed is too. No two healing journeys are the same. If I'd known what I know now, I wouldn't have waited twenty years to start my own healing process. To be fair, counseling doesn't heal an abuse victim or absolve the abuser of their wrongs. It's also hard work. Counseling equips you with the tools necessary to acknowledge, confront, and work through to live beyond your trauma. After her traumatic university experience, I'm glad Citra had immediate access to a guidance counselor and that she was believed.

CHAPTER 7

MASQUERADING

———

Becoming an attorney was not my lifelong dream. In fact, I had my sights set on a career in broadcast journalism. But, as life would have it, I met a prominent Atlanta attorney who opened my eyes to the power of the law and the need for women like me in the courtroom. I attended North Carolina Central University School of Law and served as a staff attorney with The Office of the Public Defender, Atlanta Judicial Circuit (PD's Office) for over five years. My decision to serve as a public defender was deliberate. Having survived a tumultuous upbringing, I developed resilience. And, collectively, it fed my passion for the care and treatment of individuals, especially youth, within the justice system and beyond.

What I loved most about litigation was the ability to help someone during one of the darkest times in their lives—to show up for them, see them, hear them, and acknowledge their worth. Being a youth advocate allows me to use my talents, skills, and gifts to help others every day without the back-and-forth banter with the prosecutor or trying to convince a jury or judge of my client's humanity.

Fast forward to February 7, 2017. I resigned from the PD's Office to start TSI solely guided by purpose. My good friends at Gideon's Promise came to the rescue. Jonathan Rapping, Rapp, the founder and president, and his wife Ilham Askia, Illy, the executive director, had become dear friends of mine. I consider Rapp a legal mentor and Illy a nonprofit mentor. I shared my vision with them, and they fully supported me. They even allowed me to use their office address as the physical address for TSI, where we also hosted our launch event! The ways in which this dynamic duo poured into me and TSI is invaluable.

I was hesitant to share *The Abuse Algorithm* with the world. But I did. And the response was overwhelmingly positive. Erika, the finance director of Gideon's Promise, was one of the first people to respond. I met Erika in the summer of 2012 at the Gideon's Promise Summer Training Institute. Gideon's Promise is a 50I)(3) public defender organization whose mission is to transform the criminal justice system by building a movement of public defenders who provide equal justice for marginalized communities.

Erika shared with me that I was part of one of the few classes from the Summer Training Institute where she listened to every new attorney's intro story explaining why we chose to be public defenders. She was floored by my apparent ease of sharing my story. She said she understood that my purpose was much higher than anything at Gideon's Promise, being a public defender or even what TSI could afford me.

She explained that *The Abuse Algorithm* resonated with her because it's the foundation for the greater purpose she saw for my life back in 2012. She believes *The Abuse Algorithm* will be in spaces where I may never know how it's transforming someone's life. She added that the moment she saw my post, she felt she needed to help however she could. Before she could give it a second thought, she shared the post and then messaged me directly.

I expressed my sincere appreciation for Erika's willingness to share her story with me. I encouraged her not to speak above her comfortability. She said I was one of the few people she felt like she could have this open and detailed conversation with because of my transparency.

$$t + h = 3 \ \left(\tfrac{ab}{us}\right) 3 \ \frac{a \sqrt{1g} + 0}{r^i \pm th^{(n)}}$$ **ERIKA** $$t + h = 3 \ \left(\tfrac{ab}{us}\right) 3 \ \frac{a \sqrt{1g} + 0}{r^i \pm th^{(n)}}$$

A space of my memories has been reduced. I clearly remember the grooming period, but there's a gap between the grooming period and the first time. I know I was in middle school about twelve. I was in the seventh grade. I remember him striking up conversations to get to know me. By eighth grade, he was pretty familiar. My age is one of the reasons it took me so long to give voice to the abuse. I was engaged in an inappropriate relationship. It was inappropriate because I was a child. Barely a teenager. I didn't invite this attention.

He was my teacher, my Bible teacher. I went to a very small private school. It went from first to twelfth grade, and my church was connected to it. The elementary, middle, and high schools were all on the same campus. He started grooming me in middle school, which progressed to full molestation in high school. Considering the gifts, attention, hugs, and affection, it was a full-blown relationship by high school. It was calculated. He said, "You're special. Different." He used God to control the relationship. He made himself out to be a liaison to God. Said he was protecting me from the sins of the world. It was tough to process. I had a hard time reconciling many of the thoughts he planted.

Our school was small. Most of the classes were held upstairs. Mostly, he would take me to one of the empty classrooms downstairs. Sometimes, we'd be in his car as he made stops along the way to the train station since I rode the bus to school. He'd start with, "You look nice today." He'd hug me, progressively holding me longer. He explored my body. We never had full sexual intercourse. We did everything up to it. It was happening three to four times a week, depending on when he found the space for us to be alone. It happened as often as the spirit moved him and was initiated 100 percent of the time by him.

He was a young teacher. Maybe in his late twenties early thirties. He never had children. He said it was because God didn't want him to bring a kid into this sinful world. I suspect there was a lot more to it than that. I think he got married my senior year. The abuse continued.

I didn't have one boyfriend during high school. I was sick a lot with ulcers. Mom took me to several doctors before eventually taking me to the gynecologist for the first time. I was sixteen. I told the doctor I wasn't sexually active. He didn't believe me. He gave me a pap smear. He used a large speculum. I screamed.

They hadn't allowed Mom into the room, but she came in once she heard my cries. The doctor told Mom, "She said she wasn't active, but that didn't make any sense to me. I need to see what's going on down there and why she's having all these stomach issues. She clammed up. I'm trying to get the speculum in, and she's screaming."

I thought, *This had never happened. This is unfamiliar.* My teacher drilled into my head that I should never have this experience. To me, what we did was the only thing that made sense. We never had sex. He'd insert his fingers in me. But this was my first experience with something large. It was traumatic.

Then the doctor told Mom, "Yeah, her hymen is still intact. She is telling the truth." That doctor's visit sent me into a traumatic spin. I started having more stomach issues. I was constantly sick. I couldn't eat anything. I was five-foot-six and one hundred pounds. To this day, I have not had another White male gynecologist.

Once I graduated from high school, I left the city. My teacher brought me stuff for my dorm room and even came to the city "for multiple reasons," but to bring me more stuff. It wasn't until college that I began to develop an understanding of what it was and the inappropriateness of it all. I was around more people, forming regular relationships with those my age, and I immediately realized it was wrong. I was angry. At eighteen, I cut ties with my teacher. All communication. All interaction.

My disclosure had different levels. I journaled about it—not everything, but a good portion of it. I started journaling during my junior year of high school. The first person I shared it with was a boyfriend at the time. I was about twenty-three. I gave him my journal. I still didn't have a voice for it. I wasn't ready to process it. I'd completely removed myself from that environment because it was triggering. But, some ten years later, the authorities were investigating my teacher for sexually abusing children. My case becoming local news prompted me to talk about it. Until then, my boyfriend was unaware of my experience.

My boyfriend's father was a pastor, so there was a degree of belief in his girlfriend but not a 100 percent buy-in. Because of his reaction and lack of support, it would be another five years before I spoke about my abuse again. Thoughts I'm sure he had, I had too. *Aren't abuse victims much younger than I had been? Pastors don't do that. What did you do? It's not really molestation because you were in high school. You could have said no. He wasn't holding a gun to your head or threatening you. You were an active participant.*

I'm a reader. I'd done my research. I'd heard about these things and knew it happened. But I didn't have the dynamics to be a victim, or so I thought.

My teacher never presented our interaction as a relationship. He'd say, "We have a special friendship. I'm doing this to show you how special you are." Because I'm from a big family, he'd say, "You don't get attention at home like you deserve." Traditional pedophile language.

About two years after his arrest, my teacher went to trial. Even though I was listed as a witness to testify, the statute of limitations had run for his offenses against me by the start of his trial. I was twenty-eight. Still, when he saw my name and the name of one other person on the list, he opted to take a plea. I don't remember the exact number of names on the list, but it was more than ten. I was his first. Apparently, he'd progressed to full-blown intercourse with middle schoolers by this time. Knowledge of this fact created a great degree of angst in me for not telling. I started therapy in my thirties. Full-blown processing came in my forties after the birth of my son.

My teacher had a lot of influence. He was revered. Had I told as a child, I would have been ostracized and called a liar by the church. That's why I didn't feel comfortable speaking on it until his trial. At the time of his trial, he was a principal.

He was sentenced to twelve years of probation and ordered to have no contact with children. He's a registered sex offender. He couldn't go back to teaching. He's still a pastor, though, at a different church.

I've told two of my sisters, my husband, and some friends but not my parents. My father would kill somebody. He's a protector. It would kill Mom. You have to understand my mother was raised by her grandmother. She developed tuberculosis when she was born. Her parents gave her to her grandmother to raise. Her grandmother passed when she was thirteen. At which point, Mom went to live with her parents and her siblings. She ran away and raised herself. She was taken in by the Seventh Day Adventist Church. She developed a faithfulness to them. They became her family. To this day, my mother is laser focused on life as a Seventh Day Adventist. She's obtained a certain reputation and has held leadership roles within the church. It's part of her identity. She holds them in high esteem for helping her and raising her. I grew up in the church.

Mom's allegiance to the church is one of the reasons I never told her, and maybe I'm not giving her enough credit.

She did write a letter to the school board stating that my teacher was showing me attention she didn't think was appropriate. She may have had an idea, but I don't think she understood the gravity of the situation.

I didn't share my experience with my older sister either. She's a duplicate of Mom. Super religious. Loves the Seventh Day Adventist Church. I don't have the capacity to bear their burden. I don't have the energy to nurture them through my trauma. The two sisters I have shared with try to protect me.

I saw my teacher a year ago. He gave the eulogy for one of my classmates' mom. My classmate and I were close growing up. I know I've grown and healed a lot because the sight of my teacher used to cause me physical pain. This time when I saw him, I felt nothing. For the first time in a long time. It was a win for me. He no longer had the ability to cause me pain. I feel healing is happening every day.

I don't know if that'll happen totally before I die. My pursuit of healing is a daily struggle. I've been blessed with a great husband of almost twenty years, family, and a life I honestly didn't have the capacity to dream of when I was in high school. Back then, I was just trying to get through the day. My teacher was a manipulator, a misogynist. "Don't wear this. Don't do that." He was controlling. He'd torment me if I didn't do as he said. After him, relationships were difficult. Not one positive relationship in college. My boyfriends were smart, attractive, manipulative, and super controlling. There weren't many. I can count them on one hand. And none of my relationships prior to my husband lasted more than two years. Ever.

I was determined to get help in my twenties to start the healing process. Also, at that point, the ulcers were getting worse and bleeding. It was weird. Outside of my stomach, I was perfectly healthy. But you know, trying to control every aspect of my life was a thing as well.

My parents separated about three years ago after something like fifty-four years of marriage. We went to therapy as a family. It was basically an intervention for my mom. She's a hoarder. Dad couldn't take it anymore. She's refused help in the past. During the intervention, the therapist deduced that Mom had been molested. Not that Mom had told her. She made the assessment based on her twenty-five years of experience with trauma. When the therapist mentioned it during the session, Mom instantly cried. She was already furious with us for the intervention. She wouldn't talk.

That's when I realized it was generational, another reason I'm not prepared to share it with her. I'm committed to moving forward in healing. Mom began therapy last year during the pandemic. I hope she heals too. Still, I don't know if I'll ever get to the point where I think it would be helpful to share with her.

Speaking of the pandemic, it's led to some great moments of healing. This is the greatest amount of self-care I've enjoyed my entire life. I've listened to podcasts. I took my time more. If I don't have what it takes to be the best me, I can't be the best mom, wife, sister, or friend. I've used the last year to work heavily on the inner me. I'm high functioning. Always on the go. I'm good at compartmentalizing. At any given time, I've got about twenty boxes. I know how to stop and only focus on one.

Having this conversation now is incredibly important because I wish I were able to twenty years ago. I now know that a certain amount of healing comes just from sharing. I hope my story will help someone not take twenty years to try and peel back these layers. My abuse ended thirty-two years ago. I'm still processing it. And in so many ways, I'm at the beginning. This is the first time I've shared my story with someone who wasn't close to me. I don't share my story without purpose. My story is one of my compartments I'm only open with those who I feel can pour into it or can get some type of benefit from my sharing. I'll give you a helping hand if you need it.

I have a tough relationship with the church. For the longest time, my teacher planted the seed that he couldn't resist me. To let him tell it, this connection was a special order. Something in me drew him in, pushing him to go in that direction.

Talk with your kids. My mom had five girls. Not one of us had a conversation about menstruation. Of the five, I was the one who had severe cramps, discomfort, and challenges. When I tried to give voice to that pain, it was diminished and disregarded. I was overreacting or being a hypochondriac. Literally every month, I would vomit or pass out. Mom would say, "What are you talking about? Get up and go to school."

It's unbelievable that we continue down that path. And I'm the most vocal in our family. I'm the one who gives voice, but I hated that feeling. My body was doing all these crazy things, and I had no one to guide me through it. Imagine going through puberty, the start of experiencing sensations, and you're made to feel like something's wrong with you.

I have a son. A big part of his experience will have to rely on my husband to give voice to what his body was created to do. We've taught him his body was built to have sensations, among other functions. We've explained he will experience certain urges, and that's 100 percent normal. We encourage him to lean into it. Experience it. We talk. Of course, he was super uncomfortable at first, but it lessens over time with each discussion.

These are some of the experiences that shaped my life. If your loved one has experienced something similar, understand that you can't decide when and what support looks like. You can't push it or demand it. You just have to hold space. When I fall, support me. Support me at the level, place, or emotion I am experiencing that day. Don't direct my process. You don't have to always verbalize a response or even understand. Just hold space. At fifty-one, I'm in the early stages of processing. Sharing my story for a distinct purpose is new, but I'm happy to see where it goes.

If my recollection changes, know that memories change. Many aspects of my experience I don't always remember. One space of time I've tried to put together for thirty years. For instance, I don't have a memory of the first time. Give us flexibility. Remove judgment if a memory changes. It doesn't mean it's not true. It means today, I remember something a little differently than I have prior. Don't tell me how to tell my story or pick it apart.

I don't think it ever really leaves you. It is your introduction to external relationships outside of your family. It sets the tone, so no matter how hard you try to deconstruct that negative experience, remove it, process or heal through it, it remains a part of you.

Yours in Safety, Erika

When I founded TSI, I was intentional about not saying we were founded on Christian principles. Do I believe in God? Yes. Did He anoint me for this purpose? Yes. Do I know He was my help in overcoming my experience? Absolutely! Do you have to believe in God for us to help you on your journey to healing? No. You most certainly do not. Many people have been victimized within the church. For so long, they were guilted and shamed. We will not contribute to that misguided narrative.

Still, Erika and I agree that our connection was facilitated by God. He put us together so someone else would be saved or healed at some point. Erika's learned in her relationship with God that you're not always going to understand why. Just know He's got it and the purpose is much greater than you might be able to understand. Erika's okay with that and I am too.

According to Herman Law, a law firm that exclusively represents adult survivors and children of sexual abuse, sexual abuse by clergy occurs at devastatingly high rates. Clergy sexual abuse involves abuse perpetrated by a member of a religious institution, including priests, ministers, deacons, nuns, pastors, or other clergy members. Religious institutions provide sexual predators with a unique opportunity to access and groom victims in an environment intended to be trustworthy and safe. This breach of trust is one reason why clergy sexual abuse is particularly harmful to child victims. Clergy sexual abuse was not a widespread topic of discussion in the United States for most of the twentieth century. While the egregious act happens at alarming rates, most clergy sexual abuse goes unreported and religious institutions help conceal it.

As reported by *The Boston Globe*, a shocking report documented decades-long sexual abuse perpetrated by Roman Catholic priests in the greater Boston area. According to *The Globe's* investigation, former Priest John J. Geoghan abused over 130 parishioners, most of whom were school-age boys as young as four years old, across a half-dozen Boston parishes in the 1990s. Cardinal Bernard Law, the archbishop of Boston at the time, knew of Geoghan's behavior and did not remove him from the priesthood. Instead, Law transferred Geoghan to other parishes, where he continued his abuse for years.

The Roman Catholic Church isn't the only denomination steeped in sexual impropriety. The Southern Baptist Convention and the United Methodist Church have their issues too. Most victims of clergy abuse are children. According to the National Center for Biotechnology Information (NCBI), the average clergy abuse victim is twelve. Two-thirds of those affected are thirteen years old or younger when their first encounter with sexual abuse occurs. Just over 25 percent of victims are aged fourteen years or older. In NCBI's 2019 study, 62.8 percent of victims were male, and 34.8 percent were female. (Herman Law, 2021)

Teaching children about their bodies and how to respect and care for them really is taboo in society, and I can't understand why. I have a dear friend who puts on menstrual cycle workshops for tweens because their parents either can't or don't want to discuss the topic with their daughters. I'm not sure if people think the knowledge will magically appear in their children's brains by osmosis or not. I think boys should be taught about menstrual cycles too. They have mothers, sisters, cousins, and maybe one day a wife and daughter. They should, at a minimum, understand what menstruation is, why it happens, and not be weirded out to purchase tampons and pads.

As a parent, I want my children to be well-informed. Talk with your kids about puberty before it happens. Normally, puberty starts in girls when they're between eight and fourteen years old. Most girls get their first period when they're twelve or thirteen years old, which is about two or two and a half years after they begin puberty. But some get their periods as early as age nine while others get it as late as age sixteen. In boys, puberty normally starts when they're nine to fifteen years old. On average, boys begin going through puberty a little later than girls, usually around age ten or eleven. (Nemours Kids Health, 2021)

Puberty is an awkward stage. Kids' bodies are changing, and they might feel scared, lonely, or insecure. Don't let them go through that transition alone. When you explain that it's the body's natural course and that it's perfectly normal, it can reassure your child and become a pathway to healthy, open dialogue. Answer their questions openly and honestly. If you don't know the answer, say that and then talk with someone who does. I believe despite our best intentions, parents are sometimes paralyzed by the fear of messing up their kids' lives. I know I've come down on myself at times. Push past that fear. As parents and caregivers, we must lay a strong foundation. Included in that foundation is preparedness for their body and its safety.

CHAPTER 8

COMPRESSION

———

Tasha is known as Tasha W: The Messenger of Hope. Her mission is to inspire millennial women how to rise from a place of pain to a posture of promise. She is an author-entrepreneur and transformational speaker. She applies her life experiences and educational background to help millennial women unlock the treasure that's within, confront pitfalls from the past, and explore the power of fearlessness. Tasha also founded the Royalty Refined Movement to create a safe haven for millennial women after experiencing trauma or loss.

My friend Pavielle hosts The Purpose Collective Podcast, where she empowers women of faith to uncover and pursue their purpose with reckless abandon. Tasha was her guest, and Pavielle introduced me to her. Tasha and I instantly connected. Her spirit felt familiar. She's a self-proclaimed introvert but boldly and effortlessly drops gems of how to navigate life after trauma.

According to the Centers for Disease Control and Prevention (CDC), sexual violence (SV) affects millions of people each year in the United States. The official numbers are likely an underestimate because many cases go unreported. Victims may be ashamed, embarrassed, or afraid to tell the police, friends, or family about the violence. The recurrence of victims suffering in silence is deafening. When a survivor finds their voice, listen.

$$t + h = 3 \ \left(\tfrac{ab}{us}\right)3 \ \ \frac{a\sqrt{1}g + 0}{r^{i} \pm th^{(a)}}$$ **TASHA** $$t + h = 3 \ \left(\tfrac{ab}{us}\right)3 \ \ \frac{a\sqrt{1}g + 0}{r^{i} \pm th^{(a)}}$$

I grew up in a very small community on the Eastern Shore of Maryland. Everybody knows everybody. A year and a half before I left for college, my father passed away. He was involved in a work-related incident. Because of our small-town community, Dad's death thrust our family into the spotlight—my mom, my brother, and me. My brother was twenty-one, and I was sixteen. Mom lost the only love of her life. Dad was her first everything. They had been together since high school. She was falling apart. It was bad. The news station came to our home. Representatives from Dad's job were coming by the house to get Mom to sign documents to silence her.

It was too much. I had to get away. I chose to go away to college as an escape. Ironically, I left home because I didn't want to be labeled as the girl whose father died from the explosion. Only to run away to college to be labeled as the girl who got raped. It was hard. When it happened, I didn't know what to do.

I used to be ashamed of my story. I'm not anymore.

I was a freshman in college. I didn't know my assailant personally, but we had mutual friends. So, he was around. I wasn't attracted to him and wasn't aware he was attracted to me. He and I were on the buddy system because his friend was dating one of my suite-mates in the dorm.

My assault was premeditated. He knew what he was doing. I screamed. He had duct tape to cover my mouth. I fought. He pinned my arms back. After having his way with me, he told me to zip my pants up as if nothing had happened. He said, "Don't tell anybody because I will come after you and your family. I've done this before. My dad is a cop, so I can get away with it."

The way he looked at me sent chills down my spine.

For a while after the assault, he and a group of his friends, minus the one in a relationship with my suite-mate, stalked me. They harassed me. *Who are you with? Don't tell anybody. Don't act funny.* I lived in fear the whole semester.

I was disgusted with myself. I thought it was my fault. I questioned myself. *What did you do to make him think that was okay? Was I too trusting? What did I have on to make him think this was acceptable?* I started wearing big, baggy clothes. I thought if I hid, no one else would think sexual assault was okay.

I thought I was ugly. I took all my mirrors down. I didn't want to look at myself. I was upset with myself. I blamed myself. I felt guilty, ashamed. Then I became withdrawn. I'm a personable introvert. I'm the person who checks on others when they're alone. I want everyone to be okay and feel included. That all changed. I didn't want anyone close to me or in my space. I couldn't trust anybody.

My roommate was also my best friend. After a few months, she sat me down one day and said, "What's up? You're not the same person I met at freshman orientation. What's going on?"

She thought I was still grieving the loss of Dad.

I said, "I don't know where to start."

Her reply, "Just say it. I'm not going to interrupt you. I know something is eating you up because you're not the person you were. You're not smiling. You want to be in the room all the time." She continued, "Whatever it is, I'm not going to get upset. You can tell me. I'm not going to tell anybody. I'm your best friend. I know when something is wrong."

I told her. Her mouth dropped wide open. She was livid. I had to calm her down. I told her I just needed my friend because I was already frustrated. She hugged me and said, "I can't believe this happened to you. You're one of the nicest people I've ever met." I didn't understand it either.

Then she asked, "What are you going to do with this because I don't want you to carry this. It wasn't your fault."

I looked at her quizzically.

And she repeated herself, "No, it wasn't your fault."

I told her I had no idea what to do.

Her response was, "Let's do the one thing we know how to do."

We prayed.

I agreed to pray, even though I was angry with God. I did feel better at the moment. My friend suggested I go back to what was comforting to me, journaling.

She said, "I'm pretty sure talking about it right now is too soon. Write your thoughts down, and when you feel ready, I'll go to counseling with you."

She knew I'd had a bad experience with counseling when Dad passed. The high school put me in a grief group without telling Mom. They called me down over the intercom. I didn't even want to go to school. They stared. They'd whisper, "Is she going to cry? What's she going to say? Do I mention her dad?" It was weird. Everyone knew Dad. Mom says all the time that I have Dad's heart. After school dances, we'd pile up in his pickup truck. He made sure everyone got home safely. He was involved with all my extracurricular activities.

I attend the grief group, not of my own volition. I shut down. Going to school was my way of eliminating the noise at home. Some people probably thought it was too soon for me to return to school, but Mom was crying every day. My brother was mad. I was sixteen and didn't want to hear any of it. They stuck me in a grief group with people I barely knew, expecting me to share. No, thank you.

Knowing the back story of my counseling experience, my friend was there to support me when I decided to go the semester after my assault. My assailant didn't come back the following semester. His little minions left me alone, too. But

I didn't forget. I was still hypersensitive to my surroundings. His dismissal bothered me because I felt like I didn't have any closure. It took me back to Dad. The last time I saw Dad was the night before the explosion since he left early for work.

The only reason my assailant wasn't bothering or stalking me was that he flunked out. I thought, *But for the dismissal, would he still have been carrying on the same way?* He took pleasure in harassing me. His abrupt dismissal wasn't the closure I needed. I had more thoughts than I knew how to process. I couldn't live like this. That's when I decided to go to therapy.

I was getting my strength back. I reminded myself I was loved. I was valued. This didn't define me. Each time I affirmed myself, I took my power back. I needed to be consistent. I needed to speak with a neutral party who wouldn't judge or coddle me—a person who would allow me to think and feel as I do but not give me answers they think I needed to hear.

I'm glad I gave therapy another try because it was completely different from my high school experience. Having someone listen and ask, "How do you feel today?" Having someone affirm me. Having someone say, "It's okay if some days you just don't feel like getting out of bed and other days you feel like you can conquer the world."

I attended counseling for a year and even joined a support group. It felt good to know that other people felt like I did, were experiencing the same emotions, and had the same questions. I wasn't alone. It was also good to see where everyone was in their journey and offer support. Some people were fresh, and some people had held their secret for so long.

I told Mom and my brother a year later. I told him first. Naturally, Mom felt like it was her fault. She felt like she didn't protect me. I explained to them that over the past year, I'd gone through so many processes and was now at a place of healing. Telling them was part of my healing process. It was necessary to overcome and navigate my journey.

Dad taught us to share. That's what we did in our family. We didn't go to bed upset. We had to talk about it. My brother was like, "I knew something was off. I assumed it was typical teen stuff. I didn't expect this." To this day, my brother still has a picture of him.

I'll never forget the situation, but it doesn't take precedence in my life. I'm living. I told my brother I needed him to live too. There's no hatred, bitterness, or lack of forgiveness. I've released it all. Holding on to those feelings prevented me from having healthy relationships with other people.

I used to think, *Maybe I should accept the bare minimum because I don't deserve anything else* in relationships. I thought, *My baggage is too much for someone else.* Residue from my experience remained. I made a purposeful decision to spend time in singleness to work on myself. Seven years.

I've never been as free as I am now.

I became an author and shared my story. Several people reached out to me, expressing they would have never known because of how I interact with others and how I'm a genuinely jovial person. My response was, "It happens." They shared their stories with me.

And then my brother disclosed his abuse. God used me to help him get through his pain. To be used in that way is amazing.

I found out my brother was six at the time of his abuse. Our uncle was watching him. It was our uncle's friend. My brother went to use the bathroom. Our uncle's friend followed. My brother screamed and called out to our uncle. Our uncle did not come to see about him. My brother resented our uncle for a long time but has now embraced the power of forgiveness. I finally understood why their relationship was strained. It now made sense why my brother was crazy overprotective of me. He'd held this secret for thirty-plus years.

We must normalize the conversation surrounding sexual abuse. When left unspoken, assumptions are made. When we address it and call it what it is, we can start prevention early. We grew up hearing, "What happens in this house, stays in this house." That's toxic. This way of thinking tells people to suppress their emotions. They aren't taught how to build healthy relationships or set healthy boundaries. We need to talk about CSA with the same ease as alcoholism and drug addiction.

It's not a dirty word. When you don't talk about it, it becomes dirty.

Understand that for those who have experienced abuse, healing is a lifelong process. For instance, I used to hate pap smears with a passion. I would have to talk myself off the ledge every gynecological visit. After you're raped, you get tested. My first thought was, *Lord, please don't let me be pregnant.* I did contract an STD from my assault. I was livid. I was glad it was something I could get rid of. I was glad it was not a baby.

I lived with that shame for a while. I considered myself damaged goods. I don't anymore. It was something that happened to me. It's not who I am.

Yours in Safety, Tasha

Sadly, society has normalized rape culture. Rape Culture is an environment in which rape is prevalent and sexual violence is normalized and excused in the media and popular culture. Rape culture is perpetuated by misogynistic language, the objectification of women's bodies, and the glamorization of sexual violence, thereby creating a society that disregards women's rights and safety. Instances of rape culture include but are not limited to victim blaming (*she asked for it*), trivializing sexual assault (*boys will be boys*), publicly scrutinizing a victim's dress, mental state, motives, and history, and assuming that men don't get raped or that only "weak" men get raped. (Southern Connecticut State University, 2021)

Research from the CDC shows:

- Nearly one in five women have experienced completed or attempted rape during their lifetime;

- One in three female rape victims experienced it for the first time between eleven and seventeen years old;

- One in eight female rape victims reported that it occurred before the age of ten;

- Nearly one in thirty-eight men have experienced completed or attempted rape during their lifetime;

- About one in four male rape victims experienced it for the first time between eleven and seventeen years old;

- About one in four male rape victims reported that it occurred before the age of ten.

When SV involves a victim less than eighteen years old, it is CSA. Experiencing CSA is an adverse childhood experience that can affect how a person thinks, acts, and feels over a lifetime, resulting in short- and long-term physical and mental/emotional health consequences.

Sit with those facts. As Tasha said, CSA isn't a dirty word. What's dirty is how an abuse victim feels after victimization. Imagine the smell of your assailant's breath, hair, cologne/perfume lingering in your nostrils or their body fluids leaking onto and in you. I make no qualms about Florida State University being one of the best decisions of my life. Like Tasha, I was running from home, and I ran as far as I could. How many times do we hear about young college women being sexually assaulted and being relentlessly scrutinized? And don't let the person in question be well-known, dare say, an athlete. The point I'm making is society suffers from reversal outrage. I made that term up, so follow me. The energy we put into avoiding this conversation or tearing a victim down would be better used to learn how to prevent it and better serve those who've experienced it. Period.

Girls and women are taught not to get raped. Why don't we teach people not to be perpetrators? The current ideology does not hold the perpetrator accountable for their actions. Nor does that limited way of thinking recognize boys and men as abuse and assault victims. It's equally important that we teach all youth how to protect themselves and to respect others.

CHAPTER 9

TREE TRAVERSAL

———

Tamara Hill, MS, NCC, CCTP describes intergenerational trauma, commonly referred to as generational curses, as the oppressive or traumatic effects of a historical event that are passed down to younger generations. Intergenerational problems, including oppression, can often be found in families that have been traumatized in severe forms like sexual abuse, rape, and murder. The consequences of intergenerational trauma are rarely if ever discussed unless a therapist or other mental health professional mentions it. While it is a very important topic, it's a topic that many mental health professionals are either uninformed about or simply disinterested in. Hill says that for trauma therapists, it's important to explore how trauma may have negatively impacted generations of family members.

By treating multiple clients with trauma histories, Hill underscores the impact of generation trauma. A parent or grandparent who never truly healed from or explored their own trauma may find it very difficult to provide emotional support to a family member suffering from his or her own trauma. Many families "cope" with intergenerational trauma by employing two unhealthy coping mechanisms:

- Denial—refusing to acknowledge the trauma happened

- Minimization—ignoring the impact of the trauma and making the traumatic experience appear smaller than it really is

The ways in which family members "cope" with intergenerational trauma can set the precedence for younger generations. For example, a grandparent who refused to examine the impact of her trauma may be teaching her grandchildren—intentionally or unintentionally—to ignore the impact of their trauma. Sooner or later, the trauma is likely to be triggered by something. Trauma is not something you can hide from, no matter how hard you try. (Hill, 2020)

I graduated from Louisville Male Traditional High School. I met Alex freshman year. I had a best friend. She had a best friend. We all became friends. We were the epitome of what it meant to be "Male girls." We were studious, involved in extracurricular activities, kind, outgoing, and fly.

As we became close, we learned more about each other's childhood. Alex and I traded stories in our twenties. I don't remember how it came up, probably in the context of family. As kids, we often notice the similarities and differences in our families from our friends. To this day, Alex's story is only known to a select few.

$$t + h = 3 \ \left(\tfrac{ab}{us}\right)3 \ \frac{a\sqrt{1g}+0}{r^i \pm th^{(\sim)}} \quad \textbf{ALEX} \quad t + h = 3 \ \left(\tfrac{ab}{us}\right)3 \ \frac{a\sqrt{1g}+0}{r^i \pm th^{(\sim)}}$$

My age at the time of the abuse is a blur. I attended a private school in the second grade, so I was around seven years old when it started. When the abuse stopped, I was at a different school and was about eight years old. It happened off and on during that time.

My older cousin abused me. She was either eighteen or nineteen. She lived with my paternal grandmother. My daddy's side of the family is large. Our family was routinely in and out of Grandma's house. She wouldn't abuse me every time I'd visit, but I vividly remember about four instances. Mostly, it was a random occurrence when she could get me alone, or during a couple of the times she babysat me.

The basement was the kids' domain at Grandma's house. Grownups never came down there. My cousin's room was in the attic. She'd usually do it in her room or in the basement.

Mostly she performed oral sex on me. The one time she made me perform oral sex on her, I cried. I told her I didn't want to do it. She let me stop.

One night I cried, begged, and pleaded for my mom not to let my cousin babysit me. Through tears, I told her I didn't want to go. Mom asked, "Why are you acting like that? What's wrong with you?" I couldn't tell her. Mom dropped me off.

It was dark. She set the mood. She used fans. She used ice. I lay there. She asked if I liked it. I was conflicted. It felt good. It was wrong. I was ashamed. She'd tell me it was our secret. She said that if anyone found out, we'd both get in trouble. The thought of getting into trouble wasn't what kept me from telling but the shame.

My abuser's little sister also lived at Grandma's house. She was seven, like me. Her birthday is in May, and mine is in August. One day we were all in the basement. My cousin wanted to be with me in a different part of the basement. I cried. I told her I didn't want to go. My seven-year-old cousin said, "It's okay, Alex. I'll do it." She didn't like it. She didn't want to do it. She knew how much I didn't. My little, big cousin protected me. Living with my cousin, I can only imagine how much she had to endure.

Later I found out there was so much incest and abuse on that side of the family. Grandma had nine children. Eight boys and one girl. About five of her sons had abused family members. It was a tangled web of abuse. My cousin was a victim too. She'd been abused by some of the men in our family and her stepfather. My little, big cousin had also been abused by her dad and some of our uncles. Not living at Grandma's house and my uncles' fear of Daddy is what I think prevented any of them from trying me but not her.

Another time, my little, big cousin, my brother, and I were in the backseat of Daddy's car, waiting for him to come out of the house. I don't remember where we were going. She came out to the car with cupcakes. She showed them to me, insisting I stay with her. I thought, *You cannot use cupcakes to get me to stay with you, knowing what you want to do to me.* I felt like I was her favorite. If she had a choice, it would have always been me. Only I wasn't always available to her.

Back then, I was unable to process what was happening to me. I was relieved when it stopped. I believed I was okay. Luckily for me, I was never abused again. Sometimes when a child is a victim of sexual abuse, it's almost as if people can sense their vulnerability, and they are revictimized. That's what I was most afraid of.

One day Daddy picked me up and took me to our family-owned business. He told me he needed to talk with me. We went into a back room. He sat me down. He looked me in my eyes. He held my hands and rubbed them. He asked, "Has your cousin ever touched you?" I burst into tears. I don't remember much of the conversation. I was about eight years old. After this conversation, she never touched me again.

I learned later that Daddy and Grandma confronted her. Aside from those encounters, it was brushed under the rug. We never talked about it again. I found out the reason Daddy even talked to me was that my older brother walked in on her abusing our younger brother. My older brother told Daddy, which prompted him to talk to me.

As a child, I never told anyone about the abuse. Me and my brother, who she abused, never talked about it. Although my little, big cousin and I discussed if we were gay. It's funny how you internalize things as a child. We rationalized that because we'd participated in this act with her that we were gay now. We determined this using our shared seven years of wisdom. No adult ever talked to us about these things.

Growing up, I had a male friend I would play with. We'd stand on the side of the house, and I would let him put his hands in my pants. When I was alone, I'd play with my Barbies. I'd take their clothes off and make them have sex. Sometimes with

Ken, sometimes with each other. Subconsciously, I normalized this behavior because of what my cousin had done to me.

In my twenties, I shared my story with three friends and my maternal grandmother. She helped raise me. My maternal grandmother and I were close. I remember being shocked at her response when I disclosed it to her. I expected a reaction. *Oh my gosh, I can't believe that happened to you. I'm so upset. I'm ready to go do something.* There was none. She didn't say a lot. She just asked if I was okay.

I suppressed it for so long. Once I hit adulthood, it started to resurface. I was most affected mentally and emotionally. I suffered from bouts of depression. It was difficult to process. I couldn't shake it. I couldn't rid my thoughts of the vivid images of us. I attempted therapy. I'd gone to about three sessions before I called it quits. As my therapist went deeper and challenged me, I was triggered. I couldn't take it.

My cousin eventually married a man. He had two daughters. She abused them both. She was criminally charged and sentenced to prison for abusing them. She went away for a long time. My daughter was one when she was released from prison. Her birth reignited my desire to fully process my abuse.

One day Daddy and my stepmom took my daughter to the park. One of my brothers and I met them there. My brother held my daughter as we talked. My aunt pulled up with my cousin. She was fresh out of prison. She was living in a halfway house, and my aunt had taken her shopping. My brother walked over to speak to my aunt. He still had my daughter in his arms.

At that moment, I didn't freak out. When he walked back to me, I immediately told him, "Don't you ever take my child around her. She can never see my child. She can never be around my child." He looked at me puzzled. In his defense, he didn't know what she had done to me. Daddy and my stepmom were off to the side. They heard me. They didn't say anything. I took my daughter and left.

Daddy's home is a safe space for me. We have a close-knit nuclear family. It's only when my father invites his siblings over that I'm uncomfortable. I don't want to be around them. My father has never hurt me. When he found out she was hurting me, he immediately put an end to it. Still, I don't think Daddy fully comprehends my degree of distrust and uncomfortableness with his family outside of my stepmom and siblings.

Take, for instance, one holiday Daddy had the family over to his house. She was there. He didn't tell me she was going to be there. I'd previously shared with him I didn't want to be around her. Now, we were both here. I had my daughter with me. I tried, but I couldn't do it. I left. My brother, who'd been abused by her, walked me to my car that night.

I burst into tears when we reached the car. "I don't understand why they have her around knowing what she did." I'm thinking, *He's my daddy. He's supposed to protect me. Why would he have her here?*

That's when my brother shared with me that our cousin had been abused by several different people and suffered from some mental health issues. He disclosed numerous other instances of abuse from within our family. He ended by saying, "If you're going to be mad at her, you've got to be mad at everybody because everybody's fucked up."

My brother has an exceptional ability to compartmentalize. Me, not so much. My brain doesn't operate in that way. He could separate the family from the abuse. For me, it was a tangled web of abuse. Understand that my brother and I shared our dad. His mother loves and provides for him, but she's not nurturing. He doesn't have a close-knit family on his mom's side like me.

My mom's family is healthy, loving, safe, and functional. Not to say that there aren't issues. Nobody's family is perfect. It's the family I prefer to be around. I realized Daddy's family was my brother's only family. There was no "getting away" for him.

My dad joined us outside. He apologized. He reassured me he didn't intend for me to be uncomfortable. He didn't realize her presence bothered me. I reminded him I'd already expressed this sentiment to him. By the time we made it home, Daddy had called to check on me. I broke down again. He reiterated his love for me and repeated much of what my brother had told me about my cousin when he walked me to the car.

I'm a social worker. I know "hurt people hurt people." I know that sometimes a victim can become a perpetrator. I understand some abusers don't have impulse control. I get it. I felt sorry for her.

Grandma died. At the funeral, my cousin and I spoke. We hugged. I forgave her with that embrace. Still, the sight of her was retraumatizing. There was another time Daddy wanted everyone to gather at Grandma's house. I didn't want to go. My brother asked me to come. I went for them. I went in briefly and spoke but stayed outside most of the time. I was completely uncomfortable. A few weeks later, I expressed my frustration to Daddy. I told him, "You're forcing me to be around someone who abused me. You don't know what it feels like to be violated in that way. Every time I see her, all those memories come rushing back."

And then I told him straight up, "I won't do it anymore. I've only done it for you. So, any time she's going to be around, I'd appreciate you letting me know because I won't. I will never be around her again. She will never be around my child."

I had to establish those boundaries for myself so that I could heal. What happened to her is tragic, but it doesn't negate what she did to me.

The abuse affects me the most as a parent. The love I have for my daughter. I would walk through fire before I let something happen to her. My innocence was stripped away. I was exposed to things I had no business knowing about. I won't allow anyone to snuff out the light, life, and innocence of my daughter.

I'm anxious and overprotective of her. I walk the line between having open lines of communication with her and not divulging too much. My daughter is friends with our neighbor's daughter. They played together for about a year and a half before I let her go inside their home. Our neighbor's daughter was always welcome in our home. There are very few people my daughter spends a night with. In the back of my mind I think, *You just never know.* I'm big on energy. If I get a negative vibe from someone, they won't be around my child.

I'm healing. I've come a long way, but I'm not sure I'll ever completely get over it. It's a part of me. Even though it's a struggle, I know I need to get back in therapy.

Abuse can happen to anyone. It's usually someone you know—family or friends you've known for a long time. Talk to your children. Listen to your children. Be intuitive. Pay attention to signs. If you're unfamiliar with them, educate yourself. If your child should experience abuse, learn how to help them. Don't brush it under the rug. Abuse affects a person for the rest of their life. It affects everyone differently.

Yours in Safety, Alex

Abuse can root so deeply through a family tree. I've learned that victimization is a stronghold in many families. I know it is in mine. As some family members have shared their experiences with me, I wonder just how deeply rooted our tree is. While I've never confirmed whether my abusers were victims, too, I've often wondered if they were. Though like Alex, it would not change my inclination never to want to see them again. And therein lies the problem. Family and friends who were not personally affected by abuse fail to comprehend and appreciate our position.

The family members privy to my abuse still engage with my abusers from time to time. I've expressed my disdain and confusion of their interaction with them knowing not only what they've done to me but others. My attempts were futile. I have requested that they don't invite them anywhere I am when I visit home and they don't. Part of the healing process is acceptance of what happened to us, which not everyone will understand or even attempt to.

As we continue to unravel this tangled web of abuse, we unearth more misinformation. At seven, Alex and her little, big cousin determined their experiences made them gay. It's still a common view that sexual abuse can "turn" a child gay despite no convincing or reliable evidence that premature sexual activity or CSA grossly changes sexual orientation. (Clark, 2016). But you don't know that as a child. There's a lot to learn, and we depend on our adults to teach us.

Root rot is a decaying disease that attacks the roots of trees. It can cut the life short of just about any type of tree. Moderately affected trees can sometimes be saved early on by pruning out the infected roots. However, tree root diseases are best controlled by prevention. (Elite Tree Care, LLC, 2021)

Funny how the same can be said for abuse.

CHAPTER 10

LOOPING

More than any other type of child abuse, incest is associated with secrecy, betrayal, powerlessness, guilt, conflicted loyalty, fear of reprisal, and self-blame/shame. It is of little surprise then that only 30 percent of incest cases are reported by survivors. The most reliable research suggests that one in twenty families with a female child have histories of father-daughter child sexual abuse, whereas one in seven blended families with a female child has experienced stepfather-stepdaughter child sexual abuse. (RAINN, 2021)

I met Magda through a mutual contact with the Homeland Security Investigations, New York office. One day the three of us met over Zoom to discuss how our organizations could support one another. In introducing myself to Magda, I shared that I was writing *The Abuse Algorithm*. Magda said she would like to discuss the book more later, so we scheduled a call.

Talking to Magda was easy. She was such a delight. We learned that we were both granny's babies and that neither of us wanted kids originally, but we each have a daughter and son. We basically shared our life stories. It was like catching up with an old sister friend.

$$t + h = 3 \left(\tfrac{ab}{us}\right)3 \ \frac{a\sqrt{1g}+0}{r^{1} \pm th^{(n)}}$$ **MAGDA** $$t + h = 3 \left(\tfrac{ab}{us}\right)3 \ \frac{a\sqrt{1g}+0}{r^{1} \pm th^{(n)}}$$

My mom and dad came to the US when I was two. They left my siblings and me in Guatemala with our grandmother. We lived with Grandma for five years. That's how I got so close with Grandma and my great-grandmother. We were tight. It was devastating for me when we moved to the US in November of 1971. I was seven. I think the move made me vulnerable. The natural affection parents have for their children, my father didn't have.

I can't tell you if it was in December, January, or February. I just remember it still being cold when it started.

I was ten when Grandma walked in on Dad abusing me.

I kind of put this experience out of my mind. I think God's grace allows you to forget what you can't handle. There was vaginal penetration. I don't remember the specifics, and I'm glad I don't. My mom worked nights. That's when Dad would come into my room. Mind you, I shared a room with my sister. She was a hard sleeper. I didn't make any noise. I was afraid to. The threat was, "I'll kill you and your mother." Sometimes, he would take me down to the basement. Other times we'd go to my parents' room.

Dad drank and smoked. A lot. To this day, I can't date a man who drinks or smokes excessively. The smell of the smoke and alcohol stayed with me. My father was never sober when he came to me. I understand the process of grooming and there was none. He did become physically abusive toward me. I assume to show he didn't prefer me. There were six of us, four from my Mom's previous marriage. My younger brother and I were Dad's biological children. Mom was an extraordinary woman. I loved her. It was hard for me to understand why she stayed with Dad. I'd think, *Here is this beautiful woman living with this man.* Because dad drank, there wasn't a lot of communication. We didn't bond or form a loving relationship. My grandmother, the person I was closest to and loved dearly, I'd left behind. And though I had siblings, I felt like an only child.

Mom brought all six of us to the US legally. Back then, immigration was a lot easier. Mom's employer granted her a visa, and she subsequently sent for us. I would be remiss if I didn't say Dad was very smart. I don't know what happened to him in life, but he could have been a philosopher. He would teach me math, which resulted in me always being above grade level. It was awkward. He'd teach me math by day but was doing this thing to me at night. I hated him. I had so much anger for him and nowhere to put it.

A year after we came to the US, Mom sent for Grandma. We lived upstairs. Grandma lived downstairs. I remember Grandma walking in on Dad abusing me. I don't remember everything that happened, but she told Mom. I wasn't present when she told her.

After talking with Grandma, Mom called me into her bedroom and said, "You are never to tell anyone what happened because people will look at you differently."

As a ten-year-old, I took that to mean it was my fault. There was no further conversation. Not with Mom or Grandma.

I don't know whether Mom and Dad talked about it. Later, they'd argue about it. I wanted to run away. I'd get up in the middle of the night to leave, but somebody would always be up.

I wish Mom had talked to me. I had questions. I wondered if I had a stamp on my forehead that was attracting men to me because Dad's brother surely tried.

I said to him, "I am going to tell." That's all it took.

His insistence of, "Come here, baby. Come sit over here," ceased.

I wouldn't say I was a rebel. I was an obedient child, though outspoken. I have this belief that children are supposed to be respected, and adults are supposed to show them what respect looks like. Just because you're an adult doesn't give you the right to mistreat a child. The realization that my parents aren't perfect helped me along my path. They're human. Flawed. The mere fact that they are parents doesn't give them superhuman powers. They are still susceptible to all the things we all are.

In the army, when I taught parenting classes, I would tell participants, "Don't be a bully parent."

Mom later said she stayed with Dad to punish him. Eventually, we moved to a new home, and Grandma didn't live with us anymore. I would go to her house and weep. I was about eleven. I'd say, "Please, please let me live with you."

She'd respond, "No, mama, you have to go home to your parents."

I'd ask to live with her when my parents would fight. I could hear them. Mom constantly reminded Dad of what he did to me in earshot of me. I internalized it. They fought because of me.

Now that Mom and Grandma knew, I was terrified. *Was Dad really going to kill me and Mom?* I remember he tried to slap me. I had a potty mouth. I grew up listening to old people so I could curse you up and down. This one time, if he had caught me, I don't know what would have happened. He'd knocked the lamp down trying to catch me. Mom said to him, "Go ahead. Kill her." I didn't understand sarcasm. I thought, *She wants him to kill me.*

I was an angry teen, carrying all this inside. I battled with anorexia. People who suffer from anorexia will tell you that there's a threshold, and once you pass it, there's no coming back. I went right up to it and eased back. It frightened me. I took aspirin. I'd make myself vomit and would drink gallons of water to wash it out of my system. I didn't want to die. I wanted the pretending in my home to stop. I wanted the shame to go away.

I dealt with older men. I started engaging in sexual activity at fifteen. A guy I was dealing with more than likely lied about his age. I've seen pictures of him on Facebook and thought, *Oh my God, this man is old. Back then, we couldn't have been close in age.* I thought every man wanted sex and that their interest in me was for sex. I thought I was in control, but I was a child. When older men engaged with me, they were in control.

As an adult, these pent-up emotions continued to bubble up inside me. I didn't trust my ex-husband with my daughter.

We were both military. When he would take our daughter out, I'd question her when they got back. Not overtly. It was, "Where did you go? What did you do? Did you have fun with Daddy? Did daddy play any games with you?"

I never told my ex-husband about the abuse. I couldn't share it with him. He wasn't the type of man who would have been sensitive to it. Had he known, I'm unsure of what he would have done with the information.

I was extremely careful with my kids. I talked to them early. I told them, "If anyone touches you in these private areas, you are to tell someone. And if it's me who touches you, you are to tell someone." That's how deep it was for me.

The reality is the people who have access to your children are going to be the ones you have to protect them from, not strangers. Yes, a small percentage of strangers abuse children. As a society, we want to make abusers strangers because we don't want to believe otherwise.

I was a good friend. My romantic relationships sucked. I was never present. I could walk away from anyone. While most children dream of getting married and having children, little Magda didn't.

At eleven, I said, "If I get married, I'm going to marry someone I don't love. That way, if I have to leave him, I don't care."

I have a son and a daughter. My daughter was born in Germany. She's not my ex's biological daughter. I met her father in Germany. I immediately got pregnant. He was abusive. He was six-foot-four. At five months pregnant, he held me by my neck against the wall. I never knew what made him drop me to the ground. After that incident, I never spoke a word to him again. We were stationed in the same location. I could walk into Burger King. He was going, and I was coming. He'd call my name. I wouldn't respond. He became a ghost to me. He would call, and as soon as I heard his voice, I hung up. I had my daughter alone.

I've never shared it with anyone, but I was sexually assaulted in Germany. I went on a date with a civilian guy. He assaulted me in my own home.

My daughter was about nine months old when I met my ex. We had our son three years later. I didn't want a daughter. Mom kept saying you're going to have a girl. I said, "No, Mom, in all my dreams, I am having a boy." I said, "What am I going to do with a girl?" How would I protect her? Mom couldn't protect me. I knew if anyone ever did anything to my child, I was going to go to jail. But I would never tell my daughter that. I told moms, "Don't ever tell your children you'll kill the person who hurts them because they won't tell you out of fear they'll lose you."

I didn't want kids to begin with. We grew up Catholic, and I automatically thought God was going to punish me for something I'd done. Truly, I love kids. Grandma used to babysit, and I would help her. I rationalized my punishment from God would be that because I love children, I wouldn't be able to have them.

My healing has been a long process, mostly because I kept pushing it away. Thankfully, I never got involved with drugs or alcohol. It's not my thing. Being physically active over the years has helped.

My family was still pretending like it never happened. I went along with it until my late twenties. I was living in South Carolina. I called Mom and said, "I remember."

She said, "What are you talking about?"

I repeated, "I remember. Mom, I remember. I remember what Dad did."

She said, "You're lying," and hung up the phone.

I didn't speak to Mom for a whole year. I immediately called Grandma because now I'm questioning whether I made this up. *Was it a false memory?*

Grandma said, "Honey, it's true. Maybe your mother can't handle it, but it's true. It happened."

That was the beginning of the end. I couldn't push it away as I had in my teens and early twenties. I told my younger brother in my thirties.

He said, "I'm going to kill him."

I said, "No. I think I've forgiven him, and if I've forgiven him and it happened to me, then surely you can't kill him."

But I'd repeatedly call him crying until finally, he said, "We're going to schedule a meeting with Mom and Dad."

By this time, our parents were retired, living in Guatemala. I lived in Tennessee. My brother flew to Tennessee. To my parent's credit, they came.

We sat at the dining room table. Mom and Dad sat next to each other. I sat at the head of the table. My brother sat next to me. I turned into that seven-year-old girl. I sat there, rocking. My brother looked over at me. I can't tell you what was going through my mind. I was afraid. My brother and Dad had words.

Then, I found my voice.

I told Dad, "What you did to me changed my whole life."

Dad stood up and said, "I am not going to listen to this."

That's when my brother said, "Sit down, Dad."

He sat.

I told him, "This is not going to end up as a telenovela (a Spanish soap opera). You're not going to call me on your deathbed for me to come to absolve you of what you've done. I am going to let you die and go to the hell you've had in me all these years."

Dad's head hung low.

I continued, "I have a son, Dad. How am I supposed to raise him?"

That's when Dad said in Spanish, "My daughter, what can I tell you now?"

I'd never seen my father cry.

With tears in his eyes and a pain-filled voice, he said, "You told the truth. Please forgive me."

Out of everything I'd been through, this was what always made me cry.

I knew Dad was sorry. I could tell. He never looked at me when he spoke. My parents were born in the 1930s. They weren't equipped with the tools to express their emotions. Dad was a great-grandfather to all the kids, including mine. The kids loved my dad. He tried to teach my son how to drive at two. The dichotomy was insanity for me. How was this possible? I held all this anger toward him but still saw his kindness.

When Dad owned it, I said, "Okay, it's over. We can move forward, have a real relationship."

Not this facade.

I used the opportunity to address Mom too. I told her, "What you said to me in your room made me feel like I was at fault, and you didn't leave him."

That's when she said, "I stayed with him to punish him. I wanted to see him hurt."

I told her, "Yeah, that may have been so, Mom, but what were you doing to me? I lived in fear because he said he would kill me and you. You didn't know that."

I also told them how when Mom made me iron Dad's work uniform, I'd spit on it and step on it first. I told them about the time Dad had passed out drunk on the kitchen floor, how I'd gotten the aluminum bat from the closet prepared to go upside his head. How, had my brother not walked in on me, I would have gone to juvie, and Dad would have been six feet under. Thinking back, I didn't tell my brother then why I wanted to kill Dad.

My divorce was the catalyst to the dining room table meeting. While dealing with the fallout of my marriage, the abuse resurfaced. After my divorce, I moved to California with my parents because I needed help with the kids. Living in their home at twenty-nine years old, I would be in the corner, crying, rocking back and forth. I couldn't put it away anymore.

I truly believe Dad needed my forgiveness as much as I wanted to forgive him. I am grateful my brother set the table so I could forgive my father and free myself. Shame is a coconspirator to the abuse, and silence is the glue that holds them together. The more I talked about my experience, the more I was able to shed the shame and embarrassment.

Give us the space to talk about our experience without your judgment and pity. Remind us that it's not our fault, that we did nothing wrong. We're not anomalies. This thing is real. It happens to everyone, everywhere. Talk about it. Get rid of that damn taboo! Let's talk about the experience of CSA because I think many of us have had it. We're walking around with shame, guilt, and embarrassment that was never ours to begin with.

I don't see myself as a victim or a survivor. I put it in the context of experience. When I talk to young girls, I say, "You had an experience with CSA." We can do a lot in the context of experience. You can forget it. You can put it in a mind drawer and pull it out as needed.

My experience served me well, and it made me stronger. It gives me credibility when speaking to others who share this experience and those who do not. There is no limit to my compassion, love, and empathy. I am not weak. I encourage people to use this experience as a springboard to reach unimaginable heights, not an anchor to weigh them down. We didn't choose this experience, but what we do with it is entirely our choice. I believe if you have experienced CSA, you are intended for greatness. This belief helps me move in a productive way.

As an adult, I went back to that seven-year-old. I nurtured her and forgave the adult for thinking that a seven-year-old could have done anything differently. It's been quite the journey for me. I stopped asking *why did this happen?* Or *who would I have been had I not had this experience?* I am Magda. I experienced CSA. I used to tell my kids, "A lot of people will say bad things about you, to you, but you can't be one of those people." Today, I am free. I am loved beyond my own comprehension.

Yours in Safety, Magda

RAINN (Rape, Abuse & Incest National Network), the nation's largest anti-sexual violence organization, defines incest as sexual contact between family members. Laws vary from state to state regarding what constitutes crimes of incest, CSA, sexual assault, and rape. Regardless of the law, unwanted sexual contact from a family member can have a lasting effect on the survivor.

When a perpetrator of abuse is a family member, it can be especially difficult for a child to disclose. They may care for the abuser and be afraid of what will happen to the abuser if they tell. They may have already tried to tell someone what happened, but the abuse was ignored or minimized. The abuser may have told the child that this behavior is normal and happens in all families. A child may fear getting in trouble or that the abuser will act on their threats. Sometimes a child may not know that help is available or have a trusted adult to confide in. (RAINN, 2021)

When Magda said she told her children, "If anyone touches you in these private areas, you are to tell someone. And if it's me who touches you, you are to tell someone," it hit differently. This is one time a momma bear can't be contained. I try not to keep CSA at the forefront of my mind, but I'm acutely aware of children's safety at all times. Friends and family tell me I don't have to always expect the worst. I don't. I am intentional. I observe. I ask questions. I impart knowledge. What I expect is for adults not to try a child and for a child to perceive a precarious situation.

David M. Lawson, a professor of counselor education and director of the Center for Research and Clinical Training in Trauma at Sam Houston State University, focuses his research on childhood sexual and physical abuse, complex trauma, and dissociation related to trauma. He also maintains an independent practice focusing on survivors of post-traumatic stress disorder and complex trauma.

Lawson has found that child abuse of any kind by a parent is a particularly negative experience that often affects survivors to varying degrees throughout their lives. However, incest is associated with particularly severe psychological symptoms and physical injuries for many survivors. For example, survivors of father-daughter incest are more likely to report feeling depressed, damaged, and psychologically injured than are survivors of other types of child abuse. They are also more likely to report being estranged from one or both parents and having been shamed by others when they tried to share their experiences. Additional symptoms include low self-esteem, self-loathing, somatization, low self-efficacy, pervasive interpersonal difficulties and feelings of contamination, worthlessness, shame, and helplessness.

But alas, as is so often the case, let's not forget about our boys. In 1986, David Finkelhor, known for his work on CSA, indicated that among males who reported being sexually abused as children, 3 percent reported mother-son incest. However, most incest-related research has focused on father-daughter or stepfather-stepdaughter incest (K12 Academics, 2021).

While sexual use of children by adults has been present throughout history, it has only become the object of significant public attention in recent times, since about the 1970s and 1980s. Prior to this point in time, sexual abuse remained rather secretive and socially unspeakable. Studies on child molestation were nonexistent until the 1920s, and the first national estimate of the number of CSA cases was published in 1948. (K12 Academics, 2021)

By 1968, forty-four out of fifty US states had enacted mandatory laws requiring physicians to report cases of suspected child abuse. Legal action became more prevalent in the 1970s with the enactment of the Child Abuse Prevention and Treatment Act in 1974 in conjunction with the creation of the National Center for Child Abuse and Neglect. Since the creation of the Child Abuse and Treatment Act, reported child abuse cases have increased dramatically. The National Abuse Coalition was formed in 1979 to put pressure on Congress to create more sexual abuse laws. (K12 Academics, 2021)

Harvard professor of psychiatry Judith Lewis Herman wrote the first book ever on father-daughter incest when she discovered during her medical residency that a large number of the women she was seeing had been victims of father-daughter incest. Herman notes that her approach to her clinical experience grew out of her involvement in the civil rights movement. Her second book *Trauma and Recovery*, considered a classic and ground-breaking work, coined the term "complex post-traumatic stress disorder" and included CSA as a possible cause. (K12 Academics, 2021)

In 1986, Congress passed the Child Abuse Victims' Rights Act, giving children a civil claim in sexual abuse cases. The number of laws created in the 1980s and 1990s began to create greater prosecution and detection of child sexual abusers. During the 1970s, a large transition began in the legislature related to CSA. Megan's Law, which was enacted in 2004, gives the public access to knowledge of sex offenders nationwide. Yet, with so many advances in this space, it still doesn't seem as though society fully appreciates how deeply damaging CSA is. (K12 Academics, 2021)

Part of the reason I didn't want to have children is that I didn't want to let them down or fail to protect them for any reason. You could argue that Magda wasn't protected and thus failed by her mother, father, and grandmother. I have a theory that society is conditioned to live with pain and somewhat expect it. Sometimes it's easier to ignore a situation than address it. That shouldn't be the case when it comes to our children's health and well-being. I can imagine a person would never fathom their spouse is capable of such an atrocity. But if they are, and you are aware of it, I implore you to choose your child. Immediately remove them from the situation. Contact the proper authorities. Get the child and yourself the proper medical and mental health attention. Failure to do so is to knowingly subject a child to mistreatment, at which point you become just as culpable.

CHAPTER 11

PRIVILEGE ESCALATION

___

I randomly came across Kelley's Instagram page, *Survivor-sTribe*. She recently rebranded the community's name, logo, and mission. The community is now known as *SurvivorRevive*. Anyone who knows me knows I proudly proclaim, "I'm fake on social media." To me meaning, social media is an important tool to reach a greater audience with our mission. However, but for TSI, I wouldn't have a presence on any social platform. I use the space to educate, engage and empower our supporters as well as to support others. I've met some super fantastic people on social media and Kelley is one of them.

In just two years, Kelley has curated a beautifully inclusive online community of thousands of survivors located in more than one hundred cities around the globe. It's a movement of communal support for survivors to heal, support, and empower one another. Kelley's YouTube channel hosts varying panel discussions of survivors tackling difficult topics and the latest healing modalities. I've participated in a few of her panels.

Kelley and I realized that our stories, our healing, were bigger than us. And we both decided to do something about it.

$$t + h = 3 \ \left(\tfrac{ab}{us}\right)3 \ \frac{a\sqrt{1g} + 0}{r^i \pm th^{(\sim)}}$$ **KELLEY** $$t + h = 3 \ \left(\tfrac{ab}{us}\right)3 \ \frac{a\sqrt{1g} + 0}{r^i \pm th^{(\sim)}}$$

I've experienced varying degrees of abuse from different people—sexual, emotional, and physical. The sexual abuse within the family unit was at the hands of my father. My mother was physically abusive. They were both emotionally abusive. My extended family rounded it out with invalidation and gaslighting. I've learned that abuse can be layered and it can overlap.

I have a lot of memory suppression as it relates to sexual abuse. It was probably around high school when I started feeling uncomfortable and grossed out around my father. At around twenty-five or twenty-six, I experienced my come to Jesus moment. My father came into town to go to a family friend's wedding. He stayed the night at my apartment. He slept on the couch. I remember shutting and locking my door before going to bed. I knew what the problem was. Memories had resurfaced over the years.

The sexual abuse started around four or five. I don't recall how long it went on or all that it entailed. The physical abuse went on for about sixteen years. I've experienced what's known as reactive abuse. One day I lost it and went after my mother in response to her hitting me. There was one another time when I was nineteen she gave me a fat bloody lip. I moved out.

I have no contact with my father, mother, or sister. I don't really have a relationship with the vast majority of my family, but the emotional abuse continues to this day, third-party style. Since I was a teenager, my father has been grooming our community to believe that I'm severely mentally ill. I say that sexual abuse is the perfect crime, especially if it happens in childhood. The reason being, if a child has repressed memories when post-traumatic stress disorder (PTSD) comes out, no one has any idea what the hell is going on with that child. My father used that as an opportunity to garner empathy as though he were a loving father at his wit's end because he couldn't help me. When he caused the distress. So, when I did come forward, I was met with all these barriers.

My parents split when I was about two. I don't have any recollection of them being together. Thank God because those two together were like World War III. One of my first childhood memories of them was my father trying to drown my mother in the kitchen sink by holding her head underwater.

Someone else was in the house with us—either a neighbor or a babysitter, I'm not sure. My mother told that person to take us into her bedroom and not to let my father in. My sister and I pressed our little bodies up against the door, trying to hold it shut as he tried to break it down. My father suffered from drug addiction at the time. Still, he had visitation rights.

Most of my memories surrounding the sexual abuse are fragmented. One is clear. I've learned of two other victims my father abused. Apparently, he had an accomplice. One would rape a child and then give the other access to her. Knowledge of this helped piece together a memory of my own. For years I questioned how I ended up in this one situation. My father took my sister and me out of town to Virginia under the guise of vacation. He took me to a house and left me with a man. I was there all day. I was distraught, crying. Once my father returned, he picked me up and comforted me.

I could draw you a map of what this house looks like. It was an old rickety house. It was three stories. The staircase wasn't exactly spiral but kind of turned as you walked up. For years I had this recurring dream of climbing this staircase only never to reach the top floor. But I remember what's on the top floor. The top floor resembled an attic with a pointed ceiling. An easel was in there. The man was an artist.

I was mostly alone with the man. Then his wife was there. They had a huge fight. She left. It's me and him in the kitchen. He screams at me through clenched teeth, "Right, Kelley?" He threw a sugar ball at me. It landed right in front of me. I was terrified.

My dad, sister and I were staying at this house. My father said he was taking my sister somewhere I was too little to go, but where the hell are you taking your nine-year-old that you can't take your five-year-old? My father knew what this man was capable of because he did this with him. This was also around the time my father started abusing me. I wonder if because I didn't say anything he took me to this man? I don't know if there was an exchange of money.

I always knew my father was bad, but this was next-level. I felt like I was looking into the eyes of Satan. There was no empathy. Harming me made him feel good. Where the abuse was once physical, he now employs psychological manipulation warfare. Using an old email of mine, he'd send me a birthday message every year. He would put pictures of me in there the age I was when he raped me. I'm not friends with him on FB, but he posts for my birthday like we still have a relationship. In 2017 he posted, "We're getting ready for Kelley's birthday!" I hadn't spoken to him in ten years at that point.

I grapple with the fact that I'm a product of this monster. It's bad enough what he did and then to taunt me like this.

The main memory I have of the abuse is when my sister and I would visit my father every other weekend. He lived with my grandparents. I was little, so someone was always bathing me, either my grandmother or my father. There was a light blue tiled wall in the bathroom. I recently looked the house up on Zillow, and the bathroom is the exact same. My father would turn me to face the tile. He wouldn't look me in the eye as he put his fingers in me and would touch me all over.

When I was fifteen, a friend's father molested me.

At nineteen, I was sexually assaulted on vacation in Mexico.

I come from a big Italian family, so getting your ass whooped is a normal thing. It's considered discipline. When people argue if hitting your kid is discipline or abuse, my answer is simple. It's abuse when it's not a disciplinary action, as in your child didn't do anything and you're just hitting them. If you are disciplining them, to what extent? That can also be abuse.

I had a tumultuous home life. No safe space. It's important that I recognize the people who offered support, my angels. For me, it was my boyfriend at the time. I loved him. I was about thirteen or fourteen. I grew up in Northeast Philly, which is like a conveyor belt. Everyone looks and acts the same. Same religion, Catholic. Everyone's White. I didn't fit that mold. I wanted to fit in and have friends. I met this guy. He didn't care what people thought of him. He was a self-professed weirdo. He liked art and music. He was amazing. We connected. He protected me. I was safe with him. He was a beautiful thing amid chaos.

I met up with him again in our midtwenties, and we reminisced about our past.

He said, "Kelley, I never felt so helpless in my entire life because I knew what was going on and couldn't do anything about it."

At times I would be on the phone with him, and my mother would storm in the room and start beating the shit out of me. He heard my screams. As a sixteen-year-old boy, he was hearing this and couldn't do anything about it. Who could he tell? He was Italian too.

I've only seen my mother hit my sister maybe three or four times and it was truly disciplinary in nature. Like the time she got an F on her report card, she got whooped. I have a theory about it. My sister is more amicable and gets along well with others. She's nonconfrontational. My sister is like my father in that way. My father is more of a covert narcissist. He had a softer outward personality. My mom is aggressive, angry. I'm more like Mom. I'm aggressive, assertive. Even as a kid, I was talking shit. My theory is through mom's own self-loathing, she took it out on me.

I find it difficult to trust others, but it's not directly related to grooming. It's just all-encompassing. My father's grooming wasn't traditional. It was more akin to psychological manipulations. He tried to wash away the negative memories by solely remembering the good times. He'd say, "You remember when we went miniature golfing or bowling?"

As we got older, I noticed our conversations with Dad never correlated to what was presently going on in our lives. It wasn't, "How's life? How's your partner? How's your job?" It was always remembering what we did in the past. It was weird. Now I understand why.

Catholicism was a big part of my upbringing. When I was younger, my father never went to church. He became a devout Catholic after he abused me. I'm convinced he doesn't think he did anything wrong. I don't believe for one second he was trying to find God because of his terrible deeds. I believe it was more manipulation. He needed to work on his outward perception.

Prior to my birth, my father opened a pizza shop. A couple of family members invested in it. I don't come from money, so if they gave it, it was a lot for them. But he was in a bad way with drugs, running mafia stuff, and cheating on my mom. Then he abused me. My theory is he got involved with the church to repair his reputation.

He started making us say nightly prayers. My sister is four years older than me. In high school, she'd go to parties and hang with her friends on the weekends, so it was just him and me.

One night as we were praying, he says to me, "I just thank God that I never molested you or your sister."

Years later, we were talking, and I brought this night up. I recorded the conversation. His response was, "I can understand how someone in his position would be tempted by their daughter." The audacity to put the onus on the child.

I've identified a trend with my father. He builds a crazy narrative around his victims. All our lives, he told my sister and me certain family members were crazy. It impacted my relationship with them because I was like, why bother? They're crazy. When you're young, you believe everything your parents say, and it took me a long time to piece everything together. Once I heard about the narrative that he was framing behind my back, I was like, "Oh, that's what this is."

In 2007, my father said he was moving back to Philly. By this time, my sister had two kids. I still had repressed memories. How could I say what happened, knowing I couldn't remember it all? He was going to have access to my niece and nephew. So, I told Mom and my sister about the abuse.

When I told my then partner, he was loving and supportive. I don't think I appreciated his support to the level I should have. I figured that's what people do. My expectation was that if you tell your family something terrible happened to you, they will love and support you.

When I told my mom and sister, it was awful. I wasn't surprised that mom had a reaction, but it never occurred to me that they wouldn't believe me. They didn't outright say, "I don't believe you." But for the years following, nothing changed. I had to see Dad every Christmas, every event. If I didn't come home, I'd get a ration of shit for it. When I would go, it would take weeks to get my head together after seeing him. I dealt with suicidal ideation. I was losing my shit.

My partner called my mother and told her, "You're being really fucked up right now." Which made me appreciate him more because he stood up to my mother, which I recognized was a pretty difficult thing to do.

I went through a phase of subconsciously recreating volatile dynamics in my past relationships. Not to the extent of what my parents had, but I can see now how I was limiting myself. When you're told you're unlovable, you tend to gratefully accept the bare minimum.

In 2017, I accepted a new position, a major step up. Having worked in sales for years, I was brought in to build my own department. I was winning career-wise. Normal stressors came with the job, but I started having panic attacks. I hid in bathrooms and closets so my colleagues wouldn't witness the attacks. Nothing about that job rose to this level of stress. It was my personal life. I had an epiphany. I'd worked too hard to allow anyone to mess this up for me. They had to go.

Mind you, my nephew was about to graduate from high school. I'd spent months contemplating my decision. You can't take it back. I decided to wait until after his graduation to tell my mom and sister. On the day of the graduation party, which I funded, my sister texted me. Bag in hand, I was at the door to head to the train station to go to Philly. Her text said, "Oh, by the way, Daddy's going to be here." For the first five years, after I disclosed to her and mom, they forced me to see him. Until I said I couldn't. Their solution was to make sure there was no overlap. They'd stagger our visits. He'd be there this hour, and I'd come after. We did that for another five years.

That text was my breaking point. I was over it. I regret not being able to celebrate my nephew. I didn't care about the money. She needed it, so I gave it to her. She cared so little about my well-being she couldn't even do the overlap thing.

Lack of education is a big part of the problem. I think a lot of people view abuse as a distant experience or a one-time event, not realizing it physically changes our bodies. I don't think there's a clear understanding of triggers or that we have PTSD. The other piece is that some people don't want to talk about it because it happened to them too, and they're not ready. Since I've started talking about this, I've learned about generational trauma within my own family.

Going back to my thirteen-year-old boyfriend. The relationship went from him being protective to possessive. He was becoming one of them. He was very nonconformist. He didn't want to go to prom. I was a girly girl. I wanted to get dressed up and dance. It was his prom. He didn't want to go, so we didn't. I loved him, but I broke it off. He took another girl to prom.

I lost my safe space. I didn't have family or friends who understood me. This led to my first suicide attempt. I swallowed a bottle of pills. Mom found me. She made me vomit and then sat me in a corner and berated me. She told me how stupid I was and sent me to bed. She didn't take me to the hospital. No one got me help afterward. Around the same time, I was battling an eating disorder.

My first suicide attempt I was fourteen at the end of my freshman year of high school. I turned fifteen over the summer. I moved to Virginia Beach and lived with my dad for a couple of years.

My second attempt was about two months into my sophomore year. My father found me. He tried to take me to a facility, but I talked him out of it. I told him I'd be better. I was a kid. I was terrified. I didn't want to go into a psych unit. He never got me help either. My parents had incentives not to get me help. They knew what I had to say.

Out of everything I've experienced, my parents' failure to help me after my suicide attempts impacted me the most. No matter how much someone loves me and shows me they do, I'm convinced no one cares if I die. I'll know that people care for me, but I can't feel it.

Next came hyper-sexualization. I didn't care about my body or if the people I was with cared about me. It was terrible. I started cutting school all the time. By my junior year, I started to clean up my act. I wanted to graduate. To think, I was a straight-A student until my sophomore year of high school.

In my twenties, I partied and occupied my time with friends. Being busy was best. Having fun and drinking. In my thirties, I became a workaholic. Up at 4 a.m., in the gym by five, the office by seven or eight. It was the same cycle. I wasn't living.

I'm more healed than I was in the past. I'm intentional about self-care and grounding techniques. Fitness has always been important to me. I love weightlifting. To female survivors, try the weight room. It will make you feel so powerful.

It's a journey. Find what works for you.

I started SurvivorRevive about two years ago. When #metoo came to the forefront, I said me too. I put it out on Twitter. I felt naked. I believe the universe hands you certain challenges at certain times in your life. I've had challenges where I needed to use my voice in difficult situations unrelated to abuse. Having to stand in my power triggered the desire to start talking about my abuse. It was a gradual process. I built the community by sharing my story first. It grew from there. We're thriving.

Meeting other survivors changed my life. For years, I berated myself for issues and concerns many of us deal with. For instance, not being believed and learning that unbelief is part of a bigger problem. It wasn't just me.

Words have meaning and depth, and you have to get them right.

Community is how I got to the next level of healing. I'm a hard worker. Hard work brings reward. I've educated myself to put actual terms with the feelings and emotions I was experiencing. I can have conversations with other survivors who aren't trying to change the subject, get off the phone, or simply say, "Hang in there." They get it. Communal support accelerated my healing.

I'm back in therapy. I'm reconfiguring my approach to healing. Ironically, my father and I enjoy a lot of the same things. We both like art, photography, running, fitness, and the Eagles. I'm a big football fan. For years, I've been unable to do so many things I love because of its association with him.

My therapist's response was, "What I'm hearing is that your father has stolen so much from you. Why are you going to continue to let him steal from you?"

That was my ah-ha moment.

I've decided to make a list of everything I've been missing out on. I want it all back. I'm going to revisit those things and will learn how to disassociate the things I love with him. I will live a joyful life. He stole my home. I'm moving back to Philly. He stole the Eagles from me. I'm going to the games. I'm going for long runs. I'm going to read all the books. I'm going to listen to The Doors on blast. My healing has shifted from digging into the pain he caused to living the life I want to enjoy.

Healing is akin to grieving. It's a process. There are stages of anger and pain. You feel it, but don't get stuck.

I'm Gen X. We did not have access to these resources. These conversations weren't taking place. I didn't have people to talk to, even among my friends.

If you are an ally, or you have a loved one this has happened to, do your research. Don't expect them to educate you on everything concerning their experience. Don't ask them for details. Let them share what they're comfortable sharing. Believe them. Tell them you believe them.

Check in, but don't coddle us. Discuss what happens when your loved one is in need of support. This way, you won't worry, and the survivor won't feel abandoned.

Communicate. Ask the survivor what they need from you and then provide it.

It's important to know that what we're going through is not just emotional. Our chemical makeup is different. We have things going on with our bodies that are similar to people who've fought in the war. People are sensitive to a soldier's experiences. Survivors suffer from PTSD too.

It's more than a one-time incident or something that happened thirty or forty years ago. It's something your body will never forget. Don't tell someone to get over it and move on. We can change our coping mechanisms and try to avoid triggers.

Healing for a survivor doesn't end when you've heard enough and are too sad or indifferent to deal with it.

People have accused me of playing the victim. Don't do that. It can set someone back. You're instilling shame. It can cause a person to be harder on themselves for not being further along in their healing journey. Healing is personal.

As an ally, friend, or loved one, let them go through it, offer support, and maintain your own boundaries.

Yours in Safety, Kelley

Raising kids has got to be one the toughest yet most fulfilling jobs that you may not feel adequately prepared for. Truly, there is no handbook to parenting. That aside, parents are tasked with loving, supporting, and guiding their children through change, growth, and maturity. Even if you didn't have a model of good parenting to guide you, you know what good parenting is not. It's equally as powerful. The greatest wisdom is contained within experience. (Young, 2021)

I want to protect my kids, not project upon them. Heal before having children, so your children don't have to heal from having you as a parent. I read that somewhere in passing, and it stopped me in my tracks. How many parents are doing the best they can while trying to sort through their own trauma? How many parents are parenting in the only way they know how? How many parents are operating from a space of pain?

Jim Hopper is a clinical psychologist with expertise in psychological trauma, including trauma due to child abuse and sexual assault. For over twenty-five years, he has studied traumatic memories, including recovered memories of sexual abuse.

Hopper says, "Memory is complicated. That can't be avoided. But memory can be understood."

Our brains do not simply record and "play back" events exactly as they happened in the past. Almost every instance of recall involves some processes of reconstruction by the brain, which means it involves some distortion too. Still, this does not mean that memories are "only constructions" and can't be trusted at all. (Hopper, 2021) Research suggests that some brain systems record what actually happened, and another system is responsible for how someone makes sense or meaning of what happened.

Research also shows that usually, people accurately recall the "gist" and "central details" of highly stressful experiences. For example, someone may remember who the other person was and the nature of the most disturbing sexual act or acts, and whatever it was that got their attention as it happened (i.e., the central details), but not all the furniture in a room where it happened, nor all the details of each act, especially those that they did not notice or pay attention to (i.e., peripheral details). The fact that human memory is not like an unedited video does mean that memories may not be completely accurate and that any particular memory could involve a mixture of actual and imagined events (or parts of events). (Hopper, 2021)

Of course, the picture is more complex. Someone may block out or "edit out" some disturbing emotions and sensations. Children or adults may focus their attention on a spot on the ceiling or the wall, or imagine themselves in a completely different place altogether. In those cases, the central details of the experience, for that person at that time (e.g., that spot on the ceiling), are things that would typically be peripheral details or not even part of the memory at all. Thus, what would otherwise be considered the main or most important details of the sexual acts may not be encoded into memory or only minimally so. Traumatic memories, including childhood sexual abuse, can be confusing. They can cause lots of doubts. They can trip you up. But they can be sorted out too—certainly enough to heal and have the life you want.

In working with youth over the years, I've witnessed this a lot, unfortunately. You'd be surprised how often adults/parents will discredit a child's experience if they don't remember every gruesome detail. One of the most disheartening conversations I ever had with a parent was when a mother said of her daughter, who she knew was being commercially exploited, "She will be okay." She further stated, "She'll figure it out. It happened to me and my momma too." As if CSA was a coveted accomplishment akin to three generations of educators, doctors, or lawyers. It was bizarre but not surprising.

According to Break the Silence Against Domestic Violence, a nonprofit organization providing a community of resources and support services to victims, survivors, and families affected by domestic violence, reactive abuse occurs when the victim reacts to the abuse they are experiencing. The victim may scream, toss out insults, or even lash out physically at the abuser. The abuser then retaliates by telling the victim they are, in fact, the abuser. Abusers use reactive abuse as manipulation to unfairly influence a situation. These reactions can also cause survivors to feel bad about themselves for acting against what they know to be true about themselves—that they are good, kind, capable, loving people.

Sometimes those closest to you hurt you the most. I wish it were true that all parents lifted up and supported their children. For reasons beyond logical comprehension, some people delight in inflicting pain upon others. I won't get into the myriad of reasons why. I'd like to believe that every mother or father can become a better parent. But in the event they can't, all adults surrounding children must be more aware if they are in need of help. (Birthday Wishes Expert, 2021)

CHAPTER 12

BIT MANIPULATION

——

A.K. is a fellow writer but working on a memoir. A.K. is a funny guy. We talked about his goal of becoming a gazillionaire, living in Manhattan, and attending the Knicks games every other night at the Garden. In response to me telling him I was a Lebron James fan, he quickly said he's not a fan but respects him on and off the court. A native New Zealander, A.K. had to define some of his home-grown terminology for me. It was interesting that as we spoke at 7:30 p.m. EST Wednesday evening my time, it was 11:30 a.m. Thursday morning his time. While we traded a few jokes, it didn't diminish the seriousness of our discussion.

One concept I'd like to address right now is consent. According to RAINN, consent is an agreement between participants to engage in sexual activity. Consent should be clearly and freely communicated. A verbal and affirmative expression of consent can help both you and your partner understand and respect each other's boundaries. Consent cannot be given by individuals who are underage, intoxicated, or incapacitated by drugs or alcohol, or asleep or otherwise unconscious. If someone agrees to an activity under the pressure of intimidation or threat, that isn't considered consent because it was not given freely. Unequal power dynamics, such as engaging in sexual activity with an employee or student, also mean that consent cannot be freely given.

Children can and should be taught the concept of consent early on using age-appropriate language. Intuitively, children believe what adults say and do as they are told. Without proper education, they can easily be misguided and manipulated.

In many well-documented instances, children were abused at such young ages for long periods of time and were unaware they were victims. They later learned, either through friends or other sources, that the behavior is not normal. By that time, it's too late.

$$t + h = 3 \ \left(\tfrac{ab}{us}\right)3 \ \frac{a\sqrt{1g}+0}{r^i \pm th^{(n)}} \quad \textbf{A.K.} \quad t + h = 3 \ \left(\tfrac{ab}{us}\right)3 \ \frac{a\sqrt{1g}+0}{r^i \pm th^{(n)}}$$

My abuse took place between the ages of twelve and fifteen. My abuser, Tim, lived about an hour train ride away from where I lived. I'd go visit him once every couple of weeks. Over that three-year period, I'd see him maybe once or twice a month.

I didn't know what consent was and therefore could not give it. Tim made it feel consensual. It was part of his gift, albeit a dark gift. He made "our special thing" feel normal. He assured me that this wasn't something I should fear or worry about.

Tim was a kind, welcoming person with a magnetic person-ality. If I told him to stop, he would, But he cultivated an environment where that didn't happen. You kind of always went along with what he wanted to do. I know it sounds a bit vulgar, but the only reason it didn't go all the way was that I was still a young teenager and too small. Otherwise, it would have. We did everything but that.

We started off as friends. I was twelve. Tim was in his early twenties, about twenty-three. I knew him until he was about twenty-six or twenty-seven. I met him at what would be the equivalent of what you call your summer camp. He was my cabin leader. He was fun, jovial, and bombastic. I was just so taken with him. A lot of people were. I asked for his number. I guess the seed was planted then. He was also a youth group leader at a church. He had constant access to kids.

I know other people who weren't victims but were around at the time, who later told me once it all came out, "Woah, we're so lucky because he was trying to do the same stuff with us. He tried to groom us, too."

Tim maintained the abuse under the guise of friendship. He was more than a friend to me. He was a father figure. He was extremely influential in my life, even to this day. My love for music came from him. Until meeting Tim, I liked music and was aware of it, but my taste in music was shocking. It's funny. The first cassette tape I bought was Celine Dion. She's a great singer but not exactly what you'd call world-changing or amazing music. Tim introduced me to bands like U2, The Smashing Pumpkins, Radiohead, and Massive Attack. Exposure to these artistic musicians completely changed the way I saw the world. I changed. It unlocked this creativity in my life. Radiohead is probably my all-time favorite band, and I wouldn't have known about them if it wasn't for him.

At thirteen, Dad abandoned our family. He left to go overseas. He told me he was going away for a few months for a long holiday. I was so excited about it like, "Man, that's so cool. Where are you going?" My older brother told me he wasn't coming back.

I didn't see Dad for five years—from the age of thirteen to eighteen. Subconsciously, that's how Tim became almost like a father figure. Not that he thought that, but to me, he was the only man in my life who was interested in and welcomed me. He welcomed me more than Dad. I held a special place in my heart for Tim.

Tim was never forceful. All it really took was for me to stop going to see him. One day, I was in his room. He was in a flatting situation. Flatting is when you rent a house with a bunch of other people, flatmates. Tim had his own room. I was in his room playing PlayStation. He was playing with me. I think I was just like, "Can we not?" He stopped. I think he was only interested if he was getting "consent." Maybe it made him feel wanted. It can be a turn-on for some people. I kind of just stopped going after that day. On top of that, I could see he was transitioning from me to someone else.

I later learned the person Tim transitioned to after me was a few years younger than me. He, too, was with Tim between the ages of twelve to about fourteen or fifteen. There was no overlap with us. He experienced the same kind of thing. I guess it was my time to transition away. I was lucky in a way. It could have been a lot worse.

I disclosed the abuse for the first time seven years later. I was twenty-two years old. I was watching an NBA game at my mom's house. The police called.

"This is sergeant so and so, is this A.K.?"

My immediate thought was, *Crap, what have I done? Did I not pay a fine?*

He asked if I knew Tim. I said yes. He replied by saying they'd been investigating him for abuse with kids and someone through this process mentioned my name, saying I might have been caught up in this as well.

"So, were you?"

At that moment, I thought, *Do I? Don't I? Am I ready to say?* Honestly, up until that moment, I had never once thought about going to the police. That's how I was groomed. We were friends. It was our choice.

"Yeah, it happened to me."

They got me in for a big debrief. Seventeen pages full of everything. I didn't hold back. Tim was sentenced to prison.

How has the abuse affected me beyond childhood? Name a part of my life that hasn't been affected by it. Everything. I'm only now starting to deal with it through my book and going to therapy.

When I don't know someone very well, I'm a jokester. I use humor to keep people at a distance. I'm good at it. A lot of dark humor. Recently, I've noticed as I'm writing my book, a lot more of my jokes are about pedophilia. I've got some really good ones. I guess it's a way of coping. Still, all you need to do is peel back probably one layer, and I'm on the verge of being broken again. Just by talking about stuff.

One time a colleague from HR reached out to me as a courtesy to say, "How's it going?"

I responded, "Hey, this is what I'm dealing with," and laid it all out there. I didn't mean to. I probably shouldn't have done that. It affects my life dramatically, especially with relationships, my relationship with myself, how I see myself. Really, how I don't see myself. A very strong lack of worth. It taught me that the only value I have is in pleasing someone's desires. I have become a major "people pleaser." If I'm not making somebody happy, I'm not of any value to the people around me.

In terms of healing, I'm not even there yet. I've said to my therapists and a few close friends that I have a very strong sense that I may never be healed from this. Some friends say, "That's bullshit. You can totally heal. Lots of people heal from this." Some, maybe. But I have no concept in my head of what healing means for me. I can't see it being a thing. I can see myself learning how to cope with it, finding some better habits, and learning to feel less of it. How do you un-abuse someone? How do you unring a bell?

I'm writing my book for myself. Yes, I want to help others, but my primary focus is to get this out of my system because it's been tangling me up for twenty-five years. My book is part of the untangling process. I need this. When I finish it, I'll know what I want to do with it. At least, I hope I will.

Sometimes when I write, it's hard, especially when it's graphic content. I need time to recover from it to be healthy—or to try and be healthy.

Kids are exposed to so much crazy stuff these days. You can't protect them from everything. Something is going to come across their path sooner or later. My son says heaps of kids are swearing at school. My kids know not to do it. I asked them if they did. They assure me they don't.

I tell them, "If you're going to swear, it needs to be to make a really important point!" It's just a word. It's not a bad thing. Just don't make it a habit. I tell them just because you see it in a movie or a video game or hear it from your friends doesn't mean you have to do it. I teach them that we can't tell others what to do or not to do. We can only control ourselves.

A child's innocence is supposed to be treasured and kept. It's a sacred thing. To take it away is to profane the sacred. It's a very intense form of evil to do that. To ruin the innocence of something. Treasure the innocence of our kids.

Yours in Safety, A.K.

A.K.'s story is, unfortunately, not that all uncommon. Most survivors I know had some sort of relationship with their abuser. We grappled with having voluntarily contributed to our abuse. We internalized shame from having experienced pleasure from said acts. We've spent a good portion of our lives trying to navigate it all and still live somewhat healthy, joyful, productive lives in a quest to understand who we are.

Aistear, The Early Childhood Curriculum Framework, holds that from birth, children develop a sense of who they are. Relationships with family members, other adults, children, friends, and members of their community play a key role in building their identities. Children's sense of who they are is shaped by their characteristics, their behavior, and their understanding of themselves, their family, and others. Belonging is about having a secure relationship with or a connection with a particular group of people. When children feel a sense of belonging and a sense of pride in their families, their peers, and their communities, they can be emotionally strong, self-assured, and able to deal with challenges and difficulties.

Johns Hopkins Bloomberg School of Public Health created a desk guide for organizational leaders titled, *Preventing and Addressing Child Sexual Abuse in Youth Serving Organizations.* Youth-serving organizations (YSO) are those designed in part or whole to meet children's needs and wants related to social and development enhancement, education, physical, and mental health, sports, recreation, leisure, the arts, religion, juvenile justice, and child welfare. The desk guide is a theoretical framework to place strategies for preventing and addressing CSA. The research program is ongoing to evaluate the effectiveness of the strategies.

The first practice in the desk guide addresses child well-being and safety above all else. It recognizes children benefit from caring relationships with adults. Relationships in which the adult's responsibility for a child manifests as a positive effect toward the whole child, listening, and being attentive to the child as an individual along with responding to that child's individual needs. It notes that without professionalism, caring relationships may devolve into abuse or exploitative relationships. The adults of a YSO—including leaders, staff, and volunteers—are considered professionals by virtue of their commitment to the children they serve. Professionalism within the context of caring relationships serves to maintain boundaries so that caring relationships do not become intimate relationships. Caring and professional relationships can deteriorate into inappropriate and harmful relationships through boundary violations that increase the intimacy of a relationship, as evidenced by Tim's lack of professionalism with A.K.

Stop It Now! An organization founded by a survivor of childhood sexual abuse, seeks to prevent the sexual abuse of children by mobilizing adults, families, and communities to take action that protects children before they are harmed. According to Stop It Now! sexual abuse does not occur because of a particular quality in the child but solely because of traits or decisions made on the part of the person abusing. Still, understanding why some children may be more likely to be vulnerable to sexual abuse can aid in better protection for those children.

Although the child is never the reason for the abuse, some factors lower a child's defenses against abuse and make them less able to protect themselves or get the help they could need. A few of those factors are:

- weak or absent ongoing connection to a trusted safe adult

- the child sees themselves as not deserving protection or respect

- the child feels emotionally isolated or neglected

- little or no accurate information available about what constitutes healthy touching or safe sexual feelings/behaviors

- developmental challenge or disability in the child or other family members

- child is expected to fill the emotional or intimate needs of adults

- child is a victim of physical or emotional abuse.

Kids nowadays are up against a lot. They have unfettered access to harmful information and disingenuous people with the click of a button. You'll often hear me say you can learn how to build a bomb, make a baby, or bake a cake on the internet. We live in a world where anything goes. Kids are encouraged to push and exceed the limits at all costs. Society is tolerant of inappropriateness generally.

The forty-fifth president of the United States has been accused of rape, sexual assault, and sexual harassment by at least twenty-five women since the 1970s. During his 2016 presidential campaign, a 2005 audio recording leaked of him bragging that a celebrity like him "can do anything" to women, including "just start kissing them... I don't even wait" and "grab 'em by the pussy." (Nelson, 2016)

Spoken from a true predator in chief as Dr. Stephanie Evans so accurately described him during a presentation. Sexual abuse is a top-down offense. Meaning, those in power, whether by age, status, size, or experience, take advantage of others. Therefore children and youth are innately disadvantaged.

Just as abuse victims don't get to sidestep our healing process, abusers—regardless of who they are—don't get to sidestep their wrongdoings.

CHAPTER 13

PRESSURE MODULATION

———

I first learned about David Moody when I trained to become a Stewards of Children facilitator with Darkness to Light. Stewards of Children uses real people and real stories to show you how to protect children. The framework of the training is built off the foundation of The Five Steps to Protecting Children. David was one of the survivors featured in the training materials. Having only begun publicly sharing my own story the year before, I was moved by each survivor's strength and courage. After the training, I connected with David on LinkedIn.

In 1988 David established C.D. Moody Construction Company, Inc. (CDM), an award-winning general contracting and construction management firm. CDM specializes in aviation, collegiate, commercial, K–12, municipal, nonprofit, and retail facilities, as well as historic renovations. CDM is also ranked as one of Atlanta's Top Twenty-Five Commercial Contractors and Top One Hundred Private Companies by the *Atlanta Business Chronicle*.

When David decided to publicly speak about his own childhood sexual abuse, he created Moody Speaks, a platform to help others in various stages of healing from abuse. The website provides resources, inspiration, and motivation for those on the journey to healing. David serves as a global keynote speaker discussing turning trauma into triumph through leadership, healing, and building a business while dealing with anxiety and panic attacks.

The parallels in our lives are stark. David began his entrepreneurial career in his early thirties with a supportive, loving wife, and two toddlers in tow. His personal life serves as a catalyst for his professional prominence. David inspires me. I know God is no respecter of man. As He's done it for David, He's fueling my purpose too.

$$t + h = 3 \; \left(\tfrac{ab}{us}\right)3 \; \frac{a\sqrt{1_g}+0}{r^i \pm th^{(n)}}$$ **DAVID** $$t + h = 3 \; \left(\tfrac{ab}{us}\right)3 \; \frac{a\sqrt{1_g}+0}{r^i \pm th^{(n)}}$$

I believe I was between nine and ten years old. I was groomed by a male babysitter. He was the eighteen-year-old son of our regular babysitter. He definitely seemed heterosexual. He started by showing me heterosexual porn videos and the little cartoon books they had back in the sixties. He'd tell me stories about girls he was having sex with. I didn't understand sex. I didn't have any feelings about it. Yet when he began the sexual acts, I knew it wasn't right. He threatened to hurt me if I told anyone.

The abuse happened a couple of times before my mother became suspicious. Call it a mother's intuition. She called me into her and my father's room and said, "Don't let anyone touch you." He was in our home at the time she told me this. I assume something must have transpired that gave her pause. Since he had already touched me, naturally, I thought it was my fault. I didn't say anything. This exchange is why I caution parents to be careful with what they say to children and how they approach them if they suspect abuse. Make sure the child feels comfortable and secure. I highlighted this point in my Darkness to Light video.

People like children. The abuser could be a boy or man and not necessarily gay, but they find children as easy prey. Fortunately, once my mom became suspicious, he never babysat us again. I saw him maybe two other times. Once when I was about thirteen or fourteen; by then, I was almost six feet tall. The other time I saw him was when Mom took me to his wedding. That was strange. I still can't understand her reasoning. I guess my parents probably thought he couldn't have messed with a boy if he was marrying a woman. You've got to think, this is 1965 or 1966. I buried it.

Whether abuse happens one time or a thousand times, the damage is the same when your innocence is stolen; especially if you're a heterosexual male and a male abused you. I feel it's even worse. Looking back, I realize how deeply it impacted me. In 1992 I had a complete nervous breakdown. My wife had shared with me that someone close to her had been sexually abused. I blurted it out to her. I was thirty-six years old. It was my first time disclosing the abuse. She believed me right away. She didn't question whether it was true or not.

At the time, my business was only four years old. I had suffered in silence for years. I told my wife and thought I would be done with it. There was about a two- or three-month buildup after disclosing before my first panic attack. It started off with me feeling like I wasn't in control anymore. I think finally saying it triggered the attacks. I had planned on dying with my secret. Imagine a pressure cooker. After twenty-six years of secrecy, it could no longer be contained. That same year I began therapy to understand the panic attacks and anxiety. Together my therapist and I concluded that I'd never dealt with the trauma, and it had begun to manifest outwardly. I didn't realize the depth of this traumatic experience. Still, it wasn't until late 2020 that I saw a trauma therapist and did cognitive behavioral therapy. It freed me.

Cognitive behavioral therapy is intense. You have to write down and finally deal with what truly transpired. It's a bunch of different steps. You learn your stuck points. You go through a process to free yourself. You will never forget the trauma, but you will learn to put it into perspective. I blamed myself for not disclosing my abuse and believed my failure to do so allowed him to hurt other people. Cognitive behavioral therapy taught me not to take responsibility for his actions. For fifty-five years, I did.

The abuse mostly affected my self-esteem and belief in myself. People didn't know I had to push myself extra hard to believe I could accomplish my goals. I called it imaginary fear. I was always waiting for the other shoe to drop. I lived in constant worry. I created worry. Thankfully, I never got into drinking, drugs, or any kind of wild sex stuff. I stayed busy to avoid being alone with my thoughts. Until I got married, I dated plenty of women. It was easy for me to love, yet I didn't believe I would be loved, truly. I did a pretty good job of really blanking it out. I spent all those years powering through anxiety.

Aside from therapy, exercise helps. I love hiking and nature. My photography of wildlife, nature, and helping others heal by sharing my story are equally as helpful. Most recently, I tattooed my arm with "Turn Trauma Into Triumph."

CSA is preventable. It's a topic we try to avoid because 90 percent of predators are someone close to the family or family members. Most of the time, we don't want to admit it. We say we'll keep the abuser away, yet survivors are constantly made to be around them or see them. We've got to stop being afraid to address it because it allows predators to continue doing what they do.

Normally when you see public cases like Dr. Nassar or Sandusky and others, anywhere from twenty-five to over one hundred kids are involved. They victimized children for years because nobody wanted to believe it or took the steps to stop it. A lot of families have been broken up by this. The biggest thing we've got to do is believe a child and do the proper investigation and research. I wasn't taught body autonomy until my mother got suspicious, and even then, it was no deep conversation.

I want to encourage everyone that you can turn trauma into triumph. Though we will never forget, we can have incredible lives. Get the therapy you need. To me, we get even when we become all that we can be. My goal is to create an adult advocacy center since there aren't any for adult survivors of CSA. There are great child advocacy centers. We have a bad habit of saying children are resilient, which is true, but we forget they become adults.

Yours in Safety, David

David referenced identifying his stuck points through therapy. According to Melody Jazeb, LCSW, a diplomate with the Academy of Cognitive Therapy specializing in providing cognitive behavioral therapy for people dealing with anxiety disorders, obsessive-compulsive disorder (OCD), and PTSD, stuck points are statements about yourself, others, or the world at large that are exaggerated, extreme, and often negative. Stuck points are not behaviors, feelings, facts, questions, or moral statements. They are concise statements that reflect a thought. Stuck points essentially keep you from recovering. (Center for Deployment Psychology, 2021) Much of recovery from trauma is readjusting how we relate to the world and seeing how stuck points skew reality in harmful ways.

In treatment, you focus on constructing the meaning of one's traumatic experience(s) to understand why it occurred; understand how trauma impacts one's beliefs about oneself, others, and the world at large; and identify how best to readjust one's beliefs to recognize more balanced and effective ways of thinking in the aftermath of trauma. When a person processes a stuck point, the end result helps them to reevaluate how they think of themselves and others in relation to the five core themes affected by trauma: safety, trust, power and control, esteem, and intimacy.

Jazeb offers the following example of a stuck point:

Someone may believe: "I am entirely at fault for being sexually assaulted" because of having flirted with the perpetrator prior to the assault. However, through further processing, the therapist can help the client recognize how:

- flirting is *not* an invitation to be assaulted

- there was no intention on the client's part to be assaulted, and

- the perpetrator is entirely to blame

This insight opens the door to recognize that flirting, in and of itself, is safe since it alone does not lead to assaults in other intimate settings. One can also be assisted in seeing how past flirtatious encounters did not end in an assault, to help redevelop trust in one's own judgment when considering other intimate encounters in the future. Healing is a process. When dealing with the aftermath of trauma, the right process can be freeing. (Jazeb, 2019)

I can't stress enough how much support from loved ones means to survivors. When your partner is an abuse victim, it may seem as if your need to support intensifies. As a partner or loved one, understand that you won't solve all the problems of abuse. You can listen and show your love and support. Don't try to diagnose your partner. Rather suggest they seek guidance from an expert for emotional, spiritual, and mental health support. Set healthy boundaries for yourself when your loved one shares traumatic stories of their abuse. Communicate clearly. Sometimes an abuse victim may experience intimacy issues as a result of their abuse, making their consent to participate in any form of affection paramount. Always find joy. You both deserve a life filled with it. (Henry, 2021)

As David shared about stuck points, I immediately identified some of my own. I thought about the intensity of cognitive behavioral therapy and questioned if I was ready to take that step. I know I'm most certainly not taking responsibility for my abusers' wrongdoings toward me and others. I did for a long time. I remember growing up having family gatherings and children talking to them and sitting on their laps. I would cringe. I hadn't found my voice then.

CHAPTER 14

THE PROGRAMMER

$t + h = 3$ $\left(\frac{ab}{us}\right)3$ $\frac{a\sqrt{1g}+0}{r^i \pm th^{(n)}}$ **STARR** $t + h = 3$ $\left(\frac{ab}{us}\right)3$ $\frac{a\sqrt{1g}+0}{r^i \pm th^{(n)}}$

I won't sit here and pretend that my childhood was completely horrible. It wasn't. I have vivid memories of birthday parties, sleepovers, family vacations, choir rehearsal, cheer camp, field day, BBQs, and dance recitals. We had fun.

My godmother, Shelia, had us—my big brother Tank and me—in the church from the time I was four months old. We attended every church function, and we weren't even PKs (preacher's kids). Sunday school, vacation Bible school, pastoral anniversary, choir rehearsal, usher board—you name it, and we were there. It was enjoyable because it exposed me to things I didn't see in my own home, like married parents, college-educated parents, and Black professionals from all disciplines. Church didn't just feed my soul; it ignited my thirst for more—more education, more stability, more options. Church is where I formed some of my first lifelong friendships. It didn't matter that their homes weren't like mine. When I was at church, I could forget about the hell at home and be a happy kid.

Until I turned seven, I don't recall experiencing any major difficulties in my home life. I may not have gotten a particular toy, or I remember one night Momma made me sit at the kitchen table until I ate my broccoli. I've never liked broccoli, but that was her and Tank's vegetable of choice. In a full-on protest, I quietly sat at the table staring at it. Momma and Tank had long finished eating. I was alone. After about an hour, I politely wrapped the broccoli in a napkin and put it at the bottom of the trash can. Momma later told me she knew. Normal kid woes. I'm sure real life was happening for my then thirty-year-old mother, but she was single-handedly killing it. Tank and I couldn't have been happier.

Momma worked a lot. She kept us dressed to the nines. She didn't cook on Saturday. When she wasn't working, we'd hang out, just the three of us. We'd go to amusement parks, and I'm positive that's when I developed my love of roller coasters. At Kings Island, we rode The Beast no less than four times every visit. We'd go to the movies. We saw *New Jack City*. It was not age appropriate. Momma took us to teach us what doing drugs looked like and why we, including her, could never do them. Only none of us knew this movie was a precursor for our lives.

Tank and I don't share a father, but each of them has always been in our lives. Tank calls my daddy, Daddy too. Daddy was Mr. Mom since Momma worked the third shift. Daddy combed my hair, cooked, took us to choir practice, helped with homework. I'm not sure Momma and Daddy were still romantically involved either. They're still good friends to this day. Daddy lost his mom, Nan Nan, when I was about five or six, so Grandma was like his mom too.

Momma met Brian. He randomly appeared one day. If Momma was dating, she never brought them around us. Having Brian around was new. I didn't know much about him or his family. I only ever met his one elderly aunt. Momma loved him, all of him. Even the dark parts of him she couldn't change. Brian never lived with us though he visited often.

Gradually, things changed. It became apparent that Momma was using drugs. Momma and Brian's arguments turned physical. We lived in a three-bedroom apartment. Momma was adamant that we each had our own rooms. My room was closest to hers. I always found a way to sleep in Tank's room. If there was a thunderstorm or argument going on, I'd get a free pass.

One night, they were arguing, and I was in Tank's room. Tank and I coped differently. He was strong for me. I typically was on edge, on the brink of tears. Tank was stoic. He tried to block it out. Every few minutes, I'd go ask Momma if she was okay. "I'm okay, Starr. Go back to bed, baby." They were arguing because she wanted Brian to leave. He was drunk and high.

Without warning, Momma screamed. I think Tank ran to get our uncle, who lived across the street. I ran to Momma. She was wrapped in a yellow blanket as they tussled in the middle of the kitchen. If Momma's five-six, Brian's five-three, muscular and strong. I yelled for him to let Momma go. He didn't. I don't know he heard or saw me when I grabbed the butcher knife from the kitchen drawer. He heard and saw me when the knife was to his neck.

I looked him straight in his eyes and told him, "If you don't let my momma go, I will kill you."

I meant it. He let her go. He left.

Another night, a good friend of mine was over at our house playing. She and I were super close. I left her in my room to ask Momma something. Momma's bedroom door was closed. Ordinarily, I'd knock, but that time I didn't. I walked in on Momma snorting a line of coke from a saucer on her bed. I startled her. She tried to hide it. I went back to my room and described what I saw to my friend. She said, "Starr, I think your mom is doing drugs."

Then, there was the time that Daddy, Tank, and I were sitting on the couch watching TV in the living room. Momma was at work. The apartment we lived in had a large living room with two bay windows almost the length of the wall. Tank was walking back to the couch when a brick shattered the window.

I screamed, "Tank, duck."

Thankfully, he did. The brick shattered the TV inches away from his head. Daddy ran out the front door. It was Brian. He took off.

For the next several years, Momma battled her addiction. She was a functional addict. Still, she wasn't the mom we knew. I can't pinpoint the day my abuse began or ended. I remember distinct occurrences. Unlike Erika, I didn't journal about my experiences in real time. It was a concerted effort to disassociate and suppress as much as I could.

Like Nimi, two of my abusers were brothers. Contrary to her experience, they were never with me together. For years I wondered if they discussed what they'd done to me. The oldest started first. He had long, softish fingernails that curled a bit at the tips. I feared he'd cut me when he placed them inside me. At seven, I had my first yeast infection. I don't remember the pain of the yeast infection. What I remember about it was that because of it, I couldn't take a bath with my little cousin. She's a couple of years younger than me. I spent a good bit of time at her house growing up. It's one of the places I could stay overnight. It was a safe place for me. I was devastated when her mom told me we couldn't bathe together. I cried. I thought, *It's my fault. I have this thing, no clue what it is or how I got it.* Shelia asked me if someone had touched me. I told her no. I was in enough trouble.

The abuse continued. I stayed silent.

I became a combustible vault. Not knowing that one day, all these secrets were going to break through my so-called impenetrable exterior or that I'd unwittingly give the key to an undeserving person. Either way, I was unprepared. Who was responsible for my lack of knowledge? What if the very people who were supposed to teach me were never taught themselves, resulting in generational hurt. I now know that to be the case. We were all hurting.

As Momma's drug abuse continued, I bounced around from house to house of different family members. I lived with Shelia, with Auntie Sis and Uncle Ron, and the summer before the sixth grade I moved in with Grandma. I lived with her until I graduated from high school.

For a while, only Grandma, Grandaddy, and I lived in their home. Generally, Grandaddy, Albert Davis, was a quiet, even-tempered man. He was small in stature, standing at only about five-four. He's the reason I'm short. I literally wore his khaki Dickies for my uniform in high school sometimes. Granddaddy had an eighth-grade education and worked at General Electric for about thirty years until his death.

Grandma, Maxine Davis or Mac, was a model-esque five-nine before shrinking later in life due to severe scoliosis. She was the epitome of selflessness, love, and humility. Grandma was kind, patient, and rarely, if ever, raised her voice. She always wore a smile, even during tough times. She had a quiet strength. She never complained and taught me to pray for and expect a better future. She opened her heart and home to loved ones in need.

We grew extremely close. I dubbed her "my girl." I slept in bed with Grandma until the tenth grade. Grandma and Granddaddy had long slept in different rooms. He liked to watch TV loudly all night. Grandma didn't. Grandaddy was also a functional alcoholic, and though he wasn't physically abusive to Grandma, he more than made up for it verbally and emotionally. He'd come home drunk at 4 a.m. He'd come into our room hooping and holler about nothing. In an even tone, Grandma would say, "Go on, Albert." He'd go back and forth between the two rooms until he tired himself out. Without fail, he'd get up and out of the house by 6 a.m. for work. He never missed a day.

Granddaddy passed away while I was in middle school. He hardly ever went to the doctor. Grandma took him for an eye exam, and the ophthalmologist told her to get him to the doctor immediately. Turns out, Granddaddy had lung cancer that had spread throughout his entire body. That's how the eye doctor was able to see it. Grandaddy died about two weeks later.

Grandma worked at Philip Morris as an inspector for thirty years until she retired. Nineteen of those years, she also owned and operated A&M Liquors, 18th Street's neighborhood *Cheers*. Grandma was a mother to her kids, her grandkids, her great grands, countless nieces and nephews, and anybody in need of love. I have so many great memories with my girl, like washing clothes and finding a hundred-dollar bill in Granddaddy's pant pocket. We split it, by the way.

Grandma, Shelia, and Uncle James drove me to Florida State University (FSU) in the summer of 2002. Uncle James and I had a strained relationship. When we got to FSU, he was being his usual unagreeable self. Grandma told him to go wait in the car. That was so funny. She knew I was scared. She was too. She would be miles apart from her baby for the first time. She stayed as long as she could. They had to get back on the road to Kentucky. It's anywhere from a ten-to-twelve-hour drive, depending on if you hit traffic in Nashville or Atlanta. She hugged me close and told me she loved me. She reminded me how hard I worked to get here and that I could do it. I walked her and Shelia to the car. I walked back to my dorm room head held high. Inside my room, I fell to the floor sobbing.

My roommate hadn't arrived yet. It was a good, ugly cry. I picked myself up. I prayed hard for this. FSU was the only school I applied to. It was plan A, B, and C. I never cried about being away from home again. Grandma and I talked regularly.

I went home when I could, which wasn't often. One time I'd gone home after having my angel Maxine tattooed on my back. Tank knew. Tank, Momma Grandma, and I were talking in the kitchen. Tank goes, "Grandma, what do you think about tattoos?" "They're so stupid. Why would you want to get something like that on your body?" she responded. With a sly grin, he shot back, "I don't know, Starr, why would you?" I turned to show her. She smiled brightly and laughingly said, "You're crazy, girl." I hoped it didn't make Momma feel bad. It wasn't a jab at her. Grandma was my girl. The tattoo was my way of always having her with me as she'd always been. She was present for every graduation. Attended our prewedding reception since we married in Jamaica. She witnessed the birth of both of my children. She encouraged me through law school, studying for the bar, and leaving the PD's Office to establish TSI.

Like Nancy, I was about eleven when Momma told me Daddy wasn't my biological father. The sexual abuse was still happening. The other brother mostly fondled me, kissed me, and would perform oral sex on me.

Alex gave me the courage to share that a female cousin molested me too. It was a one-off. She was older, a fully developed young woman. I still don't know why she had me take a bath with her. As we sat in the tub, she had me sit in between her legs and lie back on her. She opened my legs and massaged my clitoris. Once she finished, we washed up. We never spoke of it.

Anger nearly took up permanent residence in my heart. Why was all of this happening to me? What had I done to deserve this?

I was living a double life filled with amazing highs and crushing lows. On the outside, I was this jovial, fun-loving, happy-go-lucky girl. On the inside, I was tormented.

Why didn't my biological father want me? He'd been a close family friend, even worked at our liquor store. Why had Momma felt the need to even share that information? I had a daddy. He loved me and I loved him.

Why wouldn't my cousins leave me alone? It's wrong. It felt good. My curiosity about sex and sexuality grew. I wanted to feel good, even if it meant pleasuring myself. I'd sneak and watch *Red Shoe Diaries* or *Real Sex*. I was disgusted with myself.

Why couldn't Momma clean up her act? I never disrespected her, but some days I couldn't speak to her. I was so disappointed. She wasn't being the woman I knew her to be.

I was consumed with these thoughts, among others, all the time. As Kelley once felt, I wanted it all to end. I thought, *Would they even care if I wasn't here anymore?* I never self-harmed, though, only thought about it. At home in my safe space with Grandma, my anger was on full display. One day she checked me. She flat out told me I had a bad attitude.

My response was, "That's just the way I am."

"No," she said, "that's the way you choose to be."

The greatest words she could have spoken to me. It changed my entire outlook on life and quite possibly its trajectory. I thought *everything I'm going through sucks, but it's unfair to project it on others.* Grandma spoke from experience. I witnessed her faith, conviction, strength, and tenacity.

I chose me. I chose to commit myself to God and my education so I could get far away from Kentucky. Forever. My relationship with God is unfailing. His track record of showing up in my life is unmatched. I learned early on God was the only person I could depend on. I credit His grace and mercy for my realization because a child doesn't have the wherewithal to appreciate how significant your trust in Him truly is. Music became my outlet. I'd find songs—whether gospel, R&B, pop, or rap—to express the feelings I was experiencing.

Shelia ensured Tank and I attended the best public schools, which we call traditional schools. She found a program for any profession that piqued our interests. A college graduate, she showed me higher education was possible. Her efforts were not in vain. I excelled in school. I was heavily involved in extracurricular activities. I was on a mission.

The summer before sixth grade proved to be a pivotal point in my life. God gave me two lifelines, Grandma and Kia. Not many people can say they've known their best friend since first grade, became sisters, and have forged an unbreakable bond that's withstood the test of time and distance.

As adults, Kia and I revisited the night I disclosed to her. Our memory of the night was almost identical, only Kia remembered my actual words. I didn't. She recalls me saying, "Kia, I have to tell you something."

She casually asked, "What?" with no real expectation for what I would say because we didn't keep secrets.

I said, "You know my cousin [so and so]? He's touched me before."

Kia sat there processing. It took her a moment to respond. Confused, she asked, "What, when?"

"Like since I was little."

She apologized to me. She cried a little bit.

I cried a lot and said, "One day, I'm going to help girls like me who don't have anywhere to go and no one to protect them."

Her response was, "You can stay with me."

Kia reasoned that cousin [so and so] couldn't hurt me if I was with her. She added, "Momma will let you stay over all the time. She don't care."

I said, "Okay."

As Tasha's best friend had done, Kia remained calm and fully supported me. We went to sleep. A couple of years later, I told her cousin [so and so's] brother did it too.

Kia is still protective of me. Back then, her concern was intensified since my family was unaware of the abuse. She said she felt like it happened to her because we were so in tune. Cousin [so and so] had a habit of randomly popping up. Kia was on edge when he was around, concerned about my state of mind. She told me once I left for FSU, she finally felt like I was safe.

After I disclosed to her, Kia and I were inseparable. Her parents, Reverends Geoffrey and Deidre Ellis opened their hearts and home to me. They loved me as their own.

I became sexually active toward the end of high school. Similar to Magda, I dealt with older guys. I would tell them when and what I wanted. I figured if the sex was on my terms, I maintained control. This continued throughout college. It wasn't even about the sex. I craved being desired. My worth had become intertwined in it. How many people could I make want me and then leave? As Citra described, I spat men out. I wasn't aware of soul ties then. I wasn't concerned about a body count. This was my futile attempt to fill the void.

No one knew. I perfected the facade, flourishing on the outside and dying on the inside.

I met Devin in March 2005. I graduated that December. By the time we met, I'd decided to be alone indefinitely. No marriage. No children. It was more gratifying to focus on my education and future career.

From hello, I told Devin I wasn't interested in a situationship, relationship, or anything in between. A couple of my sorority sisters (OO-OOP) knew him. They vouched for him. We hung out. It was easy, fun. We became good friends. He's a certified goofball with a heart of gold and pure intentions. The closer we got, the more afraid I became. I was falling for him.

One time, Devin went to Louisville with me and cousin [so and so] randomly stopped by for a visit. Kia and Devin were furious. He nonchalantly strolled past us into the house. Kia was standing by Devin. You could cut the tension with a knife. Seeing Devin's face, I decided we needed to go.

Before I knew it, it was the Devin and Starr show. When we weren't in class, at work, or other commitments, we were together. I'd never felt this way about a man before. Still, I didn't know how to receive Devin's love. As David felt, I was waiting for the floor to drop out. This relationship was bound to go left. Without fail, with every elevation of closeness, I told Devin I needed a break.

I'd perfected how to be a student and professional. Romance wasn't on my radar. It'd take me years to learn I was more than a student and professional. As Erika so eloquently stated, I was a whole person.

When I interviewed Devin for *The Abuse Algorithm*, it was more of a date night. We were seated on our balcony, enjoying candlelit libations and streaming Pandora.

Devin has worked in law enforcement for the past fourteen years. Having worked with people charged with some of the most heinous crimes. Stealing a child's innocence tops his list. He recalls my disclosure to him as gradual, saying it put my behavior into perspective. Naturally, Devin is a protector. He wanted to protect me even though the damage was already done.

Devin remembers the time he saw cousin [so and so]. Out of respect for me and Grandma, he didn't say anything to him. Devin is reserved and laid back. Still, he has his limits, which is why we left the house. He said it was an altogether awkward situation; me and cousin [so and so] sharing space, me stepping in to protect him from himself when I was the one who needed the protection all those years ago. It was an interesting dynamic.

When I asked Devin how he feels the abuse affected our relationship, he said, "It's hard when you try to take on someone's pain."

Never having experienced abuse, he was torn. He wanted to protect me but wasn't sure how. He empathized. He didn't always know what to say. He felt ill-equipped at times. We both agree it has been a learning and growing process. Healing comes with growth. We grew together. We healed together.

It's no secret my childhood experiences heavily inform my parenting. I wholeheartedly agree with A.K. when he says kids are exposed to so much crazy stuff these days, and we can't protect them from everything that's out there. We can prepare them.

Devin says, "I'm very protective of our children."

We meet in the middle. We view the protection of kids through unique lenses. Our experiences shape the way we see the world.

"We're doing a pretty good job," he says.

He notes how affectionate he is with David. They hug, kiss, and David likes being close to him. His father's generation was different. He wasn't like that with Devin.

We take equal parts in maintaining our home, cooking, and parenting our children. We are raising intelligent, compassionate, self-sufficient God-fearing human beings. We model attributes we hope David and Parker will continue to embody.

Most people don't know I put Devin through the wringer. I unequivocally tried to sabotage our relationship and marriage. I had to learn how to be a good wife. I didn't feel worthy of his love. I couldn't accept him loving me for me.

A sports fanatic, when asked what advice Devin would give other significant others in his position, he likened it to a boxing match.

"It's a fight. Make a decision. Are you going to fight with your partner while they go through this, or will you fight them because you don't understand what they're going through? I hope this person is worth going through it with, especially if it's your spouse."

He continued by saying, "You take the good with the bad. Don't make it about you. It's a team effort. When you love someone unconditionally, you fight to get them the help they need. You have their back. You ride for them. Sometimes abuse victims experience people turning their backs on them or lack of support. Your behavior could further traumatize them."

He added, but not before asking if he could cuss, "Remind your partner that shit can be different. It's not all about the trauma. People genuinely love you and want to see you happy."

He ended by saying, "In a boxing match, the boxer literally has a person in their corner. As a spouse, it's your job to be in the ring, in the corner. Don't let them go at it alone. It's give and take."

He takes a drag from his cigar, puts it down, and looks at me.

"Look at the things you've helped me through. We complement one another. I saw something in you. I'm proud of your progression. It's still a battle. We've still got work to do. As long as you're fighting, I'm fighting."

I'm thankful for Devin, the man that he is. I'm thankful we were friends first. Outside of the grace of God, I feel our friendship sustained us.

Devin always said, "You were meant to be my wife. Just like you always say it's going to work out for everything else in life, I knew we would too."

I truly started loving myself at about thirty years old. I wouldn't dare bring life into this world before I was sure I could be the mother God called me to be. I thank Devin for loving me through my pain. I'm so glad God doesn't always give us what we deserve or what we think we want. Our babies will forever be my greatest accomplishments, my legacy. I'm thankful God filled my void with His love so I could love our children without restraint.

Mess is defined as a situation or state of affairs that is confused or full of difficulties. Growing up, I was definitely confused by all the difficulties I was experiencing as a child. It was all necessary, but it was tough. Have you ever prayed so hard for something you felt like you were begging? And not that you think begging is beneath you, but for whatever reason, God is not hearing you or He's not convinced of your pain?

Having learned more about Momma's upbringing as an adult, we shared more in common than I knew. Kevin and I both pieced together parts of our mothers' pasts to better understand the women they had become. I knew Grandaddy was an alcoholic. Momma witnessed Grandaddy physically abuse Grandma. He also whooped Momma and her siblings with objects other than a belt. Momma was angry with him. Growing up, she thought about hurting him. She'd talk to Grandma about it, and she would tell her, "Boo Boo," ironically a nickname Grandaddy gave her, "You don't do wrong for wrong. God will take care of it." Just as I felt about her, Momma felt as though Grandma should have been stronger and not taken the abuse because she'd done nothing wrong to deserve it.

Momma recalls the day she jumped in front of Grandaddy as he went to hit Grandma.

She says, "I took the lick for Momma. I'd been waiting on him for so long. My anger swelled to its peak. When he hit me, I hit him back. I laid him out on the floor. He didn't get up. From that day forward, I told him no more. I was moving out anyway. I'd just had Tank. We were living in a one-bedroom apartment above a liquor store, not ours. It was five kids in one room. Momma and Daddy slept in the living room."

Instantly I understood the significance of why Momma ensured my siblings and I never shared a room.

Before leaving for her own place, she told Grandaddy, "No matter where I live, if you put your hands on Momma again, I'll be back. And I'll do what you do, whoop you first and ask questions last."

Grandaddy never touched Grandma again.

In 2006, Momma and I had a breakthrough. I never disrespected her. I'd learned to love her where she was and from a distance as a defense mechanism to limit the hurt. I graduated from FSU on December 17, 2005. I spent the holidays in Louisville. After talking with Minster Dykes, I prayed and asked God to open up a time for us to talk. God interceded one day during a phone conversation. We both cried buckets. I explained to Momma how disappointed I was because I wasn't born to a mother addicted to drugs. I reminded her that my work ethic, my sense of style, my "get it done" mentality all came from her. She shared her struggles, how allowing Grandma to raise me was best and how she prayed for God to restore our relationship. Now, we're closer than close. Momma's been clean for fifteen years. We talk multiple times a day, she's one of TSI's biggest supporters, and she's a very present parent and grandparent. I made her buy an iPhone when David was born. Still, she barely knows how to work it, and he's almost eight years old. We are an example that there is another side to the pain. You go through it. You have hard, honest conversations. You rebuild.

I moved to Atlanta in January 2006. I lived with my cousin, Barry, his wife Jackie, and their son, Brandon. When I graduated from FSU, I called Barry and explained I didn't have a job, but my dream was to graduate and move to Atlanta because that's where Black people prospered. True story. Barry chuckled, saying I could, but I needed to ask the boss, Jackie. With Jackie's yes, I began a new journey in Atlanta. During the time I lived with Barry, Jackie, and Brandon, I experienced family life differently. It made me want to pattern my family after it, should I ever have my own.

I'll never forget the time I thought Jackie was dry snitching on me to Grandma. One day Grandma called me and asked why I never called Jackie on the nights I didn't come home. Having lived on my own and out of respect for Barry and Jackie, I made a unilateral decision not to come home past midnight if I was hanging out. I'd just stay with my friends. I never thought to communicate this to Jackie. What I mistook for snitching was genuine concern. From that conversation forward, I let Jackie know when I wasn't coming home. I consider myself the daughter Barry and Jackie never had. Though Barry passed away in November 2020, they both loved and love me, Devin, David, and Parker, unconditionally. They've always supported us in every way.

Atlanta was home, and I experienced several firsts there. We were married at the Newton County Courthouse in the Judge's chambers, although we recognize our wedding date in Jamaica for our anniversary. I passed the Georgia bar and became a licensed attorney. We purchased our first home. I birthed both our children at Northside Hospital. We created a life filled with love, joy, and peace. Since leaving Louisville, I've been blessed with several friends who I regard as family.

A little over the five-year mark at the PD's office, I trans- ferred from Superior Court to Juvenile Court. I represented a fifteen-year-old girl. While going over the police report with her, I inquired how she knew the man referenced in the report.

Without hesitation, she told me, "I know him from when I used to sell pussy, but I don't do it anymore."

On February 7, 2017, I resigned from the PD's office and founded TSI. My client gave me the push I needed.

Scared is not a word I would use to characterize how I felt when I decided to pursue TSI full time. Anxious. Excited. Nervous. All of which would transcend into exhaustion, isolation, and fatigue. I never speak about being overwhelmed. I vehemently rebuke the thought every time it rears its ugly head. And I instead replace it with, "Stand in the unwavering confidence that you can do anything God calls you to do, and it will be blessed."

Some call it a desire, a passion, a mission. It's my God-given purpose. And while I can't pinpoint the exact moment I fully accepted my calling, I know my unwavering trust in Him blossomed at the tender age of seven. Looking back, my trust grew from utter desperation, but thankfully, He takes us as we are.

Everything happens for a reason. Nothing is by chance. Take my name, for instance. It's thirty letters long. Momma named me Shavontana MargieMoin-Starr Davis (pronounced sha·von·ta·nay mar· ge· morn· ing). Daddy made up my first name. Grandaddy gave Momma my middle name, telling her that if she gave me that name, I wouldn't want for anything. It was a nod to his Native American ancestry. My family has called me Starr since birth. I joke with Momma all the time that it should have been my first name. Unbeknownst to us, Granddaddy was on to something.

I chose the name The Starr Institute because everyone has a light inside of them and if given the opportunity to shine, they will. Our slogan is *Shine Where You Are* because there will be hard times in life, but even then, we shine.

A week after I resigned from the PD's Office, Grandma was diagnosed with stage four cancer of the duodenum. It's a rare form of cancer of the upper small intestine. Doctors gave her six months to live. We made a pact that we were going to fight for her life and my purpose.

There wasn't a single time in my life that I needed Grandma that she wasn't there for me. The more I reflect on the woman she was, the more I realize I'm more like her than not. I've always described myself as the life of the party—outgoing, fun-loving, loud, never met a stranger kind of girl. Grandma was meek, conservative, and quiet. I'm more like her in the most important ways. She was a woman of strong faith. I watched her fight battles on her knees in prayer and at the dining room table during Bible study my entire life. She was a forgiver. Growing up, I'd tell her all the time, "You give too much. You shouldn't give if they're unwilling to help themselves. You shouldn't give to your detriment." She said I'd understand when I had my own children. She explained that even Grandaddy was hurting. He'd experienced a volatile upbringing, and he didn't have the tools to work through it.

She was an encourager. There was never a time I shared a goal with her that she didn't immediately affirm it. Followed by instructing me to buckle down, study, practice, and research, etc. Grandma was a giver. She would literally give you the shirt off her back. I joked and called our house the *do drop inn* because at some point, a loved one was bound to be down on their luck, and they knew Mac always had space. She was full of joy. She didn't complain. She was too busy reminding us how good God was to ever stay down for too long.

What do I find myself doing? Trusting God in every area of my life, giving myself time limits to be in my feelings when disappointments happen. At a young age, I decided God was the only person I could totally depend on. I love hard. I probably forgive too easily. Devin says I'm loyal to a fault, which allows people to hurt me. Like Grandma, I genuinely look for the good in everyone. It's there, sometimes buried under turmoil, hurt, and pain. If you're feeling down and want to stay down, don't call me! I am going to find the good in every situation and tell you how awesome you are in the process.

She was an entrepreneur. Having left their hometown of Columbia, Tennessee, Grandaddy and Grandma began their family in Louisville, Kentucky. Though she worked for Philip Morris for thirty years, she owned and operated A&M Liquors (the liquor store) for nineteen years.

When Grandma ran the liquor store, we never called her an entrepreneur. She certainly didn't refer to herself as one. She didn't talk to me directly about owning a business either. But I watched as she would wake up early to go open the store. When she made the calls for inventory, I listened as she negotiated the price. I watched as she took pride in the appearance of the store, inside and out. I noted how she interacted with customers—the old faithful and the newcomer. I watched her close down and count the books. I observed how she managed my momma, uncles, and others who worked there. She transformed a neighborhood with a pool table, dart machine, and jukebox. The liquor store was a safe place for the neighborhood to convene. A place to let their hair down after a long day's work. It honestly was a place where everyone knew your name. We celebrated life and mourned the loss of friends and family there. The liquor store was an extension of our home.

My girl hung in there for a solid three years after her cancer diagnosis. On Friday, January 31, 2020, I loaded the kids up in the car headed to Kentucky to see about her. Tank called me several times, saying I needed to come home to see Grandma. If I'm being honest, part of me was dreading it because I felt like it would be the last time I would see her on this side of heaven. During the latter part of 2019, Grandma's health rapidly declined. She was experiencing more pain, less mobility, and extreme weight loss. She never carried a lot of weight. Momma prepared me for how small Grandma had gotten. Her arm was the size of Parker's.

Still, my girl was in her right mind. When I walked into her room, peace fell over both of us. I acknowledged she was waiting for me, and she acknowledged this was the hardest thing I'd had to do in life. I immediately crawled into bed with her. I didn't leave her side that weekend. We prayed. We laughed. Parker did her sight words for her. We talked. I told her I was at peace, and she had to be at peace. For once, she had to put herself first. Even though she knew, I reminded her that everything I am is because of her. I thanked her for taking me in, for loving me, for always being there for me, for showing me how to love God more than anything, for showing what faith in action truly means. I tried not to cry too much. My angel was transitioning to receive her actual wings. It didn't matter that she was confined to her bed or that we had to change her. She drank some water. She didn't eat.

I'd never seen Grandma in so much pain. Her fingers and feet turned purple. I rubbed them until the color came back until it didn't. I was scared. I wanted to call 9-1-1, but Momma said I couldn't because Grandma was in hospice at home. I called the nurse. I don't remember her name, just her heart. She was kind and gentle yet straightforward. She evaluated Grandma and then asked to speak with us in the living room. She explained that the noise I described Grandma making the night before was known in the medical community as the death rattle. She spouted off more information. I stopped listening after she said Grandma probably had about twenty-four to forty-eight hours to live. I didn't sleep much Friday or Saturday because Grandma didn't. She was racked with pain. I stayed at her bedside. Saturday afternoon, she said she wanted to sit in her reclining chair. We hugged while she was in the chair. I was on my knees, leaning over the arm of the chair in her embrace. She said she wanted to take a nap. When I tried to pull away, she hugged me tighter. Auntie Sis offered me a pillow for my knees. We slept like that. What I wouldn't give for her to hold me again. To laugh with her, to hear her say, "Hey, girlfriend." I'll never forget the sound of her voice.

On Sunday, I delayed leaving as long as I could. Atlanta is a six-hour drive from Louisville. At about 2 p.m., me and the kids had to go. Family and friends were coming by the house in droves to see Grandma. I laid my head on her chest for what seemed like forever and cried like a baby. Shelia was sitting at her bedside. She was crying. Grandma was a mother to her too. I told Grandma I loved her. I couldn't say goodbye because I knew this really was goodbye. I said, "I'll call you when we get home." The kids slept most of the drive. We made it home at about 8:45 p.m. I fed and bathed the kids. During their prayers, Parker said, "Thank you, God, for healing Nana." They were in bed by 9:45 p.m. Exhausted, I plopped down on the floor and turned the Superbowl on with a little over a minute to go. I needed a distraction. Within moments, my little sister, Ayanna, called saying Grandma was gone. In true Grandma fashion, my girl made sure we got home safely.

A piece of me died that day.

When I think of Grandma's life, I am reminded of 2 Timothy 4:7, "I have fought the good fight, I have finished the race, I have kept the faith."

This book is a collection of truths. Kevin's truth. Nimi's truth. Nancy's truth. Citra's truth. Erika's truth. Tasha's truth. Alex's truth. Magda's truth. Kelley's truth. A.K's truth. David's truth. My truth. We experienced it. Lived through it. We overcome it daily. We aren't anomalies. That's what saddens me most.

As a survivor, it never ceases to amaze me how blame is quickly shifted to victims. Somehow, despite the unavoidable circumstance, it's their fault. This is especially heartbreaking when it comes to children. A child is to be loved. A child is to be fed, clothed, educated—protected. And protected by whom? Well, in some cases, protected by the very predators who snatch away their innocence and violate their sense of safety.

Let me say this... at *no* point is it ever okay to question *why*, *how*, or *when* a victim discloses. You weren't there. You didn't experience it. You haven't been held captive by their violation. Instead, embrace them for where they are in the process— mentally and emotionally. Embrace them for their strength to stand in their truth—no matter how unpopular or painful. Know that not every victim reacts the same. And know that because we are all different, we all have different ways and means of coping with the hardships of life. Not everyone has someone to talk to. To confide in. To trust.

Make no mistake about it—this is a form of trauma in its purest form. And this trauma transcends into every area of life. If left unchecked, it can manifest mentally, physically, and emotionally. Know that some victims wish this wasn't a part of their story. Know that some victims speak up for others who may never find the courage, or never have the outlet to utter their truths. Know that *we* survived something no child should ever have to endure. So, know that if *we* choose to speak, there's not a day that goes by that the turmoil of *our* past still lurks over our shoulder.

I told Momma, Grandma, and Shelia about my abuse twenty-one years after it happened. *Twenty-one!* And you know what? After twenty-one years, to speak it meant I had to relive the pain, shame, anxiety, and disgust.

Writing was a beloved pastime of mine growing up. When life got too hard, I stopped. In the last few years, I asked

God to rekindle a love that once was. He allowed me to see a video on LinkedIn of a lady detailing her experience with Georgetown Professor Eric Koester's Book Creator's Institute. I checked it out. The opportunity was inviting. It was the right time. This book has lived inside me for almost my entire life.

My faith is my greatest asset, and my ability to cultivate community is a close second.

Pastor Steven Furtick said, "Faith and fear are both a product of your focus, and you can choose either one at any moment in your life."

I choose faith every time. Knowing God takes faith, focus, and follow-through. My experience was the cost of purpose. I no longer begrudge it. Pastor Sarah Jakes Roberts said I have to burn who I became to survive so I can encounter who God said I need to be to thrive.

Today, I am a wife, mom, attorney, speaker, and youth advocate. Cycles can be broken. I'm striving for global generational healing. It's attainable, and it starts with protecting our young people. We must improve our response to reduce CSA, develop empathic reactions toward survivors, foster more positive attitudes toward helping them, and mandate visible policies and training for physicians, nurses, and teachers. We need to change the stigmas surrounding this issue on a national level, recognizing the racial and gender disparities, too.

From a cultural perspective, secrets are literally killing the Black community. Generational poverty. Generational trauma. Generational abuse. Passed down from parent to child. How do we overcome the literal weight of a sometimes harsh, unrelenting world that loathes our very existence? It's almost as if Black people are assigned trauma as a birthright.

Healthy, thriving children and youth should be the rule, not the exception.

What I love most about working with young people is witnessing a child find their voice. When they realize their worth and tap into their potential and embrace how truly amazing they are. When they understand they are not what happened to them and are not defined by their worst mistakes. Sometimes children and youth can't find the words, so I'll continue to speak up in those times.

Maya Angelou, one of my favorite authors, was also sexually abused as a child. Using one of her quotes, I replaced the word woman with survivor. "Each time a survivor stands up for themselves, without knowing it, possibly, without claiming it, they stand up for all survivors."

Will you join me in standing up for our children and youth?

Yours in Safety, Starr

CHAPTER 15

REVERSE ENGINEERING ABUSE

———

I attended a training titled, "Can You See Her? The Criminalization of Women and Girls in Human Trafficking." Dr. Kanathy Haney was the facilitator. After the event, I introduced myself. I explained to her I was new to South Florida and sought to connect with individuals and organizations to best serve the needs of our children and youth. Dr. Haney also introduced me to several individuals with whom TSI could partner.

$t + h = 3 \ \left(\frac{ab}{us}\right)3 \ \frac{a\sqrt{1g}+0}{r^i \pm th^{(\infty)}}$ **DR. HANEY** $t + h = 3 \ \left(\frac{ab}{us}\right)3 \ \frac{a\sqrt{1g}+0}{r^i \pm th^{(\infty)}}$

Dr. Kanathy Haney, PhD, CHES, CPH began her career in child welfare as a social worker in 2007. Her first field assignment was child abuse investigations. While she loved working with families in need of immediate help, she questioned whether this field was for her.

She transitioned to an organization providing children with counseling, case management, placement, and licensing for foster homes. She's facilitated individual and group counseling sessions. She specifically worked with children needing a higher level of foster care due to their psychosexual analysis of whether they themselves had been abused or had abused other children.

During her field assignment, Dr. Haney developed a desire to become a clinical social worker and do clinical therapy. She wanted to help kids work through trauma. While working for a group foster home, she worked with kids of varying age groups. She conducted individual and group therapy. She taught them life and communication skills and healthy relationships. It wasn't long before she experienced burnout. She wanted to start her own foster home seeing firsthand the many flaws within the system and the inability to fix them in her current role.

For instance, when kids would go on runaway status, they reported it to the sheriff. Dr. Haney's first instinct was to go look for the child, but this was not procedure. It was difficult for her to separate emotionally. She was in her early twenties. The concept of trauma-informed care wasn't widely known or practiced back then. She switched to the public health and promotion realm to focus more on prevention and healthy living with the intent of preventing kids from getting into abusive situations. She wanted to study having a healthy lifestyle and a healthy family. She deduced if we provided children and families with healthy exercise, nutrition, drug prevention, and high-risk sexual behavior education we could prevent it. The end goal was and still remains to make kids and families healthier.

She went on to obtain a master's degree in exercise science and health promotion and her PhD in Public Health. Though out of the field of child welfare, she remained an active volunteer in the community working with children and is currently a health professor.

Some eight years ago, Dr. Haney viewed a short human trafficking video and was given some follow-up materials. As a social worker, she'd heard about human trafficking, but like most people, it was hard to wrap her head around it initially. She was compelled to learn more. She joined Rescue Upstream a nonprofit organization providing in person and online outreach related to human trafficking. She's served as the Chair of the Human Trafficking Coalition at Palm Beach State College for almost seven years. Regarding human trafficking, she's done research with the University of Florida as part of the prevention and solution efforts locally and nationally. She also presents with the American Public Health Association.

When asked about her experience working with child sexual abuse victims, Dr. Haney spoke globally. It's different depending on their age range, but working with teenagers proved to be more difficult. Typically, they don't always want to talk or share. Kids in middle and high school are primarily influenced by their peers. You build a rapport for them but must also maintain your professional boundaries. Their acceptance of you is key to making an impact. Whether it's young kids, teenagers, or adults, my approach is always to meet them where they are, especially for the more challenging individuals. I am nice but stern, a transferable skill I developed working with older people in the hospitality industry during my first jobs.

Over the years, I've developed close relationships with the kids. I have observed they prefer to speak with the same person they have come to trust. They aren't keen on forced relationships, even in a clinical capacity. As professionals, we have to determine whether it would be more beneficial for an individual to work with someone else, which can be difficult on some clinician's pride. Clinicians need to learn not to take things personally from clients as they are going through trauma, which brought them to you in the first place.

Lack of trust is common among kids experiencing sexual abuse or human trafficking. Maslow's hierarchy of needs theorizes food and shelter among the categories of needs. Many kids in foster care are without their basic needs and may now have them barely met. Their new home is not necessarily better than previous situations. They've experienced varying levels of trauma. You treat them on a case-by-case basis, but clinicians must remember most kids do not want to be in their new placements and have difficulty adjusting. Acting out and various maladaptive behaviors should be expected and understood, not punished. Of course, appropriate boundaries should be in place but through a trauma-informed lens.

Kids' behaviors vary. Those who've experienced a lot of traumas may appear angry, quiet, or withdrawn. People process trauma differently. Depending on how much trauma they endured, kids can develop defense mechanisms making it harder to get through to them. Sometimes we mistake trauma for troubling behavior. It should serve as a red flag to be more attentive in trying to speak with the child to figure out what's going on. If a child is acting out often, there's a reason. It is the professionals' duty to attempt to better understand and facilitate that child's needs.

We live in an environment where we punish people for their behavior. Instead, try utilizing a trauma-informed approach to establish the root cause to better help the person. We often see people masking their trauma with substance abuse. Child sexual abuse survivors can act out more sexually too. These are points of consideration whether a professional is working directly with individuals or from a more preventative capacity. Professionals will have to work to connect and build meaningful relationships with abuse survivors. Prevention is paramount because it can affect a child's life and their relationships forever.

HEALTH ISSUES

When asked about the health issues child sexual abuse survivors experience, she began with mental health issues including depression and anxiety. She explained that some kids develop dissociative tendencies. It occurs when they try to disassociate from what was happening in the moment so as not to feel the pain. In severe cases, it could trigger dissociative identity disorder or multiple personalities.

Of course, abuse survivors are prone to different STDs, HIV, and early pregnancies. This is another reason that reproductive health professionals should be more educated on abuse and know when there may be red flags to further investigate. There's a wide range of physical health issues, sometimes traumatic brain injuries from being hit. Ultimately, it impacts their relationships, their quality of life, daily functioning capabilities and may cause PTSD. Numerous abuse survivors develop PTSD. Complex PTSD (CPTSD) is not in the Diagnostic and Statistical Manual of Mental Disorders (DSM). The DSM is the diagnostic manual used for mental health and diagnoses codes as well as differential diagnoses. Complex PTSD is seen in causes of repeated victimizations and abuse of various traumas.

I hope complex PTSD is more identifiable in the DSM the next time it's edited and that CPTSD is added. PTSD can be debilitating. Sometimes it's harder to diagnose and treat people who have mental health issues. As professionals and community members, we need to be more aware of it. PTSD or other mental health symptoms can also lead to poor physical health issues and more chronic diseases due to long-term bodily inflammation. High levels of stress can lend itself to heart disease and diabetes as well as putting someone at risk for a wide range of conditions such as substance abuse.

TREATMENT
When asked about forms of treatment for abuse survivors, Dr. Haney says people respond to different things. A trauma-informed approach requires a therapeutic modality unique to them. It could be yoga, art, or psychotherapy (talking). Although since psychotherapy can be triggering, therefore, it is not always the best to use initially when a clinician is aiming to decrease symptoms and calm the nervous system. This fact reiterates the need for therapists to be trauma-informed.

There are specific types of therapy. I'm a fan of cognitive behavioral therapy. There's also a more trauma-focused cognitive behavioral therapy. Understandably, individuals who've experienced these traumas have certain thoughts about themselves, others, and their relationships with the world. The more rational a person's thoughts, the better they're potentially going to feel as our thoughts lend to our emotions. Depending upon our experiences, we might be more fearful of a lot of things in life, which could lead to more negative thoughts that could hamper our emotions and self-esteem. I favor cognitive behavioral therapy because it promotes more positive talk and reframing cognitive distortions. Our thoughts impact our emotions.

Incident reduction therapy is used as a desensitization method. It's when a person repeatedly talks about the event to become desensitized. It's not good for everybody. It's not my preferred modality, but it works. Again, current nervous system functioning must be considered as it may not be the best for someone currently experiencing a high level of symptoms. Overall, the individual should be consulted and allowed to choose which treatment modality may be for them.

Eye Movement Desensitization and Processing (EMDR) is good for PTSD and trauma. I haven't done it personally. Individuals that have experienced a lot of trauma report it was painful afterward as they could feel the trauma in certain parts of their body. One survivor reported feeling like she'd gotten hit by a train the next day. She had to take ibuprofen and was very drained.

Brain spotting is built on the EMDR. Individuals report no negative physical impacts afterward. They handle the processing of trying to find the trauma in the body differently.

However, a limited number of providers conduct brain spotting currently.

Lastly, though not widely researched, people other than sexual abuse survivors have had good experiences with binaural beats. Binaural beats based therapy requires a person to wear headphones. A different frequency is played in each ear, causing a specific brainwave to occur. Some give you more focus, while others are more calming if you experience anxiety. Essentially, different kinds of brainwaves coincide with some aspect of functionality. This could be contraindicated in certain cases of seizures or TBI, although it has also been shown to be helpful in these instances, so it must be monitored.

VISION

When asked the future she envisions for the prevention of child sexual abuse, Dr. Haney wants age-appropriate sexual abuse, human trafficking training, prevention, and drug education starting as early as preschool. There needs to be a requirement within the educational system as well as having parents educated from preschool to learn where to get help. Perhaps a requirement for preschool licensing.

Many times, in child welfare cases, drugs are involved. Drug treatment is necessary. Although we have more counselors in schools now, we still need more mental and physical health courses to educate kids and parents. I'm joking partly when I say parents should be shown a parenting video at the hospital after birth prior to discharge. Being a parent is the single most important as well as the hardest job in the world, and we don't get a manual. We expect everyone will know what to do and how to handle themselves. I've also noted that many abusers were abused themselves, so there's a generational element to this too. However, not everyone who is abused becomes an abuser.

Until we start to look at abuse holistically, it'll be harder to prevent and treat. Making kids more aware as well as teaching them healthier boundaries and consent are beneficial. Having somebody they can talk to is also necessary. A lot of times they won't talk to their parents. When I work with parents, I encourage them to make sure their child has someone to talk to if they can't personally be the one their child talks to, like an aunt or uncle, an older sibling, a cousin. They need somebody. If they don't have somebody, they may find the wrong somebody who could potentially take advantage of or hurt them.

We have to start being more proactive in this field instead of being reactive. A lot of times, adults are struggling with substance abuse and mental health too. In the United States, one in twelve people over the age of twelve are on antidepressants. Think about how many people are not being treated or who self-medicate on top of those who consume alcohol because it's socially acceptable.

We need to have these conversations freely. We're getting better, but we still have plenty of room to grow. I'm happy with the progress being made, but we still have significantly more work to be done. Having these conversations with parents, kids, and schools—including colleges—will move the proverbial needle. We also need to fund better programs for people who have been victimized and are trying to cope with the aftermath.

We need an improved child welfare system and more funding to pay employees. There's high turnover due to low pay, high caseloads, excessive hours, high stress, high trauma, and secondary trauma. It is hard to operate in a trauma-informed manner under those conditions. We also need evidence-based programs.

The juvenile justice system also needs an overhaul. Many in the juvenile justice system have been abused sexually and physically. Most of them come from homes with substance use. Kids are being arrested at thirteen and becoming entrenched in the system while experiencing further trauma. We need to do better about not treating kids like criminals but rather helping them work through their traumas. In most cases, children do not belong in the typical criminal system. Actually, most people do not, but that is a different conversation about ending mass incarceration. We need to be more trauma-informed, and most people need mental health services and true rehabilitation.

You can spend years treating people in a positive way that's going to make them more productive in society anyway. If we are to be global citizens, we should want everybody to be their best selves.

———

Writing this book, though necessary, was hard. I've experienced every emotion imaginable. I unlocked hidden parts of my heart as I became transparent, vulnerable, and truthful.

I hope that you will use our experiences as a reference guide to protect young people. My intent was not to scare you but to inform you.

You were warned this would be a hard read. Now it's time to just sit with it. Reflect upon the stories shared. Take into consideration we are all doing the best we can in life. When we know better, we can do better.

Make the necessary changes and adjustments.

Extend yourself and others grace.

I felt compelled to share my story because, truly, it was cathartic. Above my own healing is my hope to inspire others to overcome their traumatic experiences.

Brené Brown said:

"Owning our story and loving ourselves through that process is the bravest thing we'll ever do."

Will you be brave in the relentless pursuit to protect young people from abuse?

THE ADVERSE CHILDHOOD EXPERIENCES QUIZ

The American Society for the Positive Care of Children (American SPCC) provides the following free quiz on their website to determine an individual's ACE score.

THE ACES QUESTIONNAIRE

	For each "yes" answer, add one. The total number at the end is your cumulative number of ACEs.		
	Before Your Eighteenth Birthday:		
1	Did a parent or other adult in the household often or very often... a) Swear at you, insult you, put you down, or humiliate you? or b) Act in a way that made you afraid that you might be physically hurt?	YES	NO
2	Did a parent or other adult in the household often or very often... a) Push, grab, slap, or throw something at you? or b) Ever hit you so hard that you had marks or were injured?	YES	NO
3	Did an adult or person at least five years older than you ever... a) Touch or fondle you or have you touch their body in a sexual way? or b) Attempt or actually have oral, anal, or vaginal intercourse with you?	YES	NO
4	Did you often or very often feel that... a) No one in your family loved you or thought you were important or special? or b) Your family didn't look out for each other, feel close to each other, or support each other?	YES	NO
5	Did you often or very often feel that... a) You didn't have enough to eat, had to wear dirty clothes, and had no one to protect you? or b) Your parents were too drunk or high to take care of you or take you to the doctor if you needed it?	YES	NO
6	Were your parents ever separated or divorced?	YES	NO
7	Was your mother or stepmother: a) Often or very often pushed, grabbed, slapped, or had something thrown at her? or b) Sometimes, often, or very often kicked, bitten, hit with a fist, or hit with something hard? or c) Ever repeatedly hit over at least a few minutes or threatened with a gun or knife?	YES	NO
8	Did you live with anyone who was a problem drinker or alcoholic, or who used street drugs?	YES	NO
9	Was a household member depressed or mentally ill, or did a household member attempt suicide?	YES	NO
10	Did a household member go to prison?	YES	NO

WHAT DOES YOUR SCORE MEAN?

The quiz score is based on ten types of childhood trauma measured in the ACE Study.

Five are personal—physical abuse, verbal abuse, sexual abuse, physical neglect, and emotional neglect.

Five are related to other family members: a parent who's an alcoholic, a mother who's a victim of domestic violence, a family member in jail, a family member diagnosed with a mental illness, and the disappearance of a parent through divorce, death, or abandonment.

You get one point for each type of trauma. The higher your ACE score, the higher your risk of health and social problems.

As your ACE score increases, so does the risk of disease, social and emotional problems.

With an ACE score of four or more, things start getting serious. The likelihood of chronic pulmonary lung disease increases 390 percent; hepatitis, 240 percent; depression, 460 percent; suicide, 1,220 percent.

The most important thing to remember is that the ACE score is meant as a guideline: If you experienced other types of toxic stress over months or years, then those would likely increase your risk of health consequences.

Fortunately, our brains and lives are somewhat plastic, which means our mental and physical health can improve. The appropriate integration of resilience factors born out of ACE concepts—such as asking for help, developing trusting relationships, forming a positive attitude, listening to feelings—can help people improve their lives.

HOTLINES, LINKS, &
SUGGESTED READINGS

———

THE CHILDHELP NATIONAL CHILD ABUSE HOTLINE
1 (800) 4-A-Child or 1 (800)422-4453

https://www.childhelp.org/hotline/

**THE NATIONAL CENTER FOR MISSING
AND EXPLOITED CHILDREN**
1-800-THE-LOST

https://www.missingkids.org/gethelpnow/cybertipline

The CyberTipline is the nation's centralized reporting system
for the online exploitation of children.

DARKNESS TO LIGHT
https://www.d2l.org/

866.FOR.LIGHT or Text Light to 741741

Call if you have encountered child sexual abuse and need resources or support.

RAINN (RAPE, ABUSE & INCEST NATIONAL NETWORK)
RAINN is the nation's largest anti-sexual violence organization. RAINN created and operates the National Sexual Assault Hotline.

https://www.rainn.org/

800-656-HOPE (4673)

BOOKS:
The Body Keeps the Score: Brain, Mind and Body in the Healing of Trauma by Bessel van der Kolk, MD

Girls Like Us by Rachel Lloyd

My Grandmother's Hands: Racialized Trauma and the Pathway to Mending Our Hears and Bodies by Resmaa Menakem

ACKNOWLEDGMENTS

I'd like to acknowledge those who have given this book, and the stories within it, a heart for sharing, loving arms to embrace community, and legs strong enough to move forward in healing:

Kevin, Nimi, Nancy, Citra, Erika, Tasha, Alex, Madga, Kelley, A.K., David, Dr. Haney

To the Abuse Hackers, your support made this book's publication possible:

Todd Beaman	Brittany Barnes
Sarah Martin	Margie Gill
Serena Nunn	Sharon Clark
Danielle Paul	Zanele Ngubeni
LaKisha Jones	Rabiatu Barrie
Jamal Davis	Tamela Holland
Kelvin James	April Swain
Gary Ross	Nicole Merenivitch

Wendy-Ann Dixon

Romaine Harris

Gary Hawkins

Dewayne Roberts

Phillip Grimes Jr.

Kiana Davis

Aristea Williams

Kendra Thurston

Andre Sullivan

Kirisha Snow

Marlin Jenkins

Eunice Davis

Nefertara Clark

Ryann Hallback

Robyn & Antoine Woods

Todd Rutledge

Deirdre Ellis

Meghan Callier

Devin P. Davis Sr.

Debontina Adamson-White

Tavares Hampton

Jessica Walker

Giselle Balfour

Marcus Davis

Sharnell Myles

Ju'Riese Colon

Marina Sampanes Peed

Joshua Gilbert

Arthur Lemons Jr.

Brandon Baxter

Akela Crawford

Taniesha Alexander

Nicole Cumberbatch

Trish Miller

David Roth

Alyn Goodson

Hazina Alladin

Ria Story

Carol Bowman

Kristina Newton

Tiffany Roberts

Erika Lamb Berrien

Rronniba Kamarakafego

LeTizia Smith

Martina Esparza

Melanie Thompson

Kia Samuel

Chaqueva Robinson

Torris Butterfield

Chrystal & Darnell Mote

Latora Francis

Dwight Sweeney II

Arrington & Roseline
Watkins

Carolyn Amos

Tranae Rey

Juana Jones

Asha Brewer

Taneishia Fields

Rochelle Lyles

Jennifer Swain

Kelly Prejean

Kenneth Walker Jr.

Devin Davis Jr.

Lacey Doyle

Takiesha Matthews

Apphia Maxima

Tawanna Hopson

Takeshia Jackson

Jenille Morgan

Thomas White

Jonathan Rapping

Marcus Davis

Ayanna Davis

Kimberly Myers

Liz Head

Kesha Walker

Amy Shipp

Lawrence & Charlene Green

Samantha Graber

Shauna Hill

Ashlee Thomas

Giget Johnson

Morris Thorpe

Jacquelyn Martin

Eric Koester

Kelley Taurino

Kisha Malone

Brandy Johnson

Lynn Larose

Sidney Minter

Shelia Thompson

Jeffrey Brown

Tova Palomino

Danielle Davis

Janelle Williams

Tiffany Wright Ousley

Cindy Noble

Angela Hite

Ashley and Jeremane
Blackwood

Jacquelyn Baxter

Melba Robinson

Otis Ferguson

Akia Ellis

Taija Kelty

Tie Velasco

Tyderrick Davis

Whitney Frye

Sheri Hart

Nefertara Clark

To the visionary, Eric Koester, my amazing editors, Michael Bailey, Shawna Quigley, and Sandy Huffman, and the entire Creator Institute and NDP, thank you for community.

To my alpha readers Dr. Samantha Graber, Dr. Giselle Balfour, and Melba Robinson, thank you for your time and invaluable insight.

APPENDIX

INTRODUCTION

Avila, Lorraine. "Y'all Don't Want to Talk about This, But We Must: Sexual Abuse in Black and Brown Communities." *Latino USA*, July 15, 2020. https://www.latinousa.org/2020/07/15/abuseinblackbrowncommunities.

Center on the Developing Child at Harvard University. "Resilience." Accessed October 24, 2021. https://developingchild.harvard.edu/science/key-concepts/resilience.

Darkness to Light. "Child Sexual Abuse: About the Issues." Accessed August 28, 2021. https://www.d2l.org/child-sexual-abuse.

Houston, Pam. "The Truest Eye: Toni Morrison." *O, The Oprah Magazine*, November 2003. Accessed October 27, 2021. https://www.oprah.com/omagazine/toni-morrison-talks-love/all.

Laymon, Kiese. *Heavy*. New York: Scribner, 2018.

Murray, Laura K., Amanda Nguyen and Judith A Cohen. "Child Sexual Abuse." Child and Adolescent Psychiatric Clinics of North America 23, No. 2 (April 2014): 321–37. https://www.ncbi.nlm.nih.gov/pmc/articles/PMC4413451.

RAINN (Rape, Abuse & Incest National Network). "Children and Teens: Statistics." Accessed October 24, 2021. https://www.rainn.org/statistics/children-and-teens.

Shared Hope International. "What is Sex Trafficking." Accessed October 24, 2021. https://sharedhope.org/wp-content/uploads/2017/07/What-is-Sex-Trafficking-Printable-Handout.pdf.

CHAPTER 1—ADVERSE CHILDHOOD EXPERIENCES

Block, Robert MD. "Long-term Consequences of Childhood Abuse." *Virtus Online*, Accessed October 27, 2021. https://www.virtusonline.org/virtus/free_article.cfm?free_articles_id=608.

Burke Foundation, The. "Adverse Childhood Experiences (ACEs)." Accessed October 24, 2021. https://burkefoundation.org/what-drives-us/adverse-childhood-experiences-aces/.

Burke-Harris, Nadine. "How Childhood Trauma Affects Health Across a Lifetime." Filmed September 2014 in San Francisco, CA. TEDMED 2014 video, 15:29. https://www.ted.com/talks/nadine_burke_harris_how_childhood_trauma_affects_health_across_a_lifetime.

California Health and Human Services Agency. "Dr. Nadine Burke Harris." Office of the California Surgeon General, Accessed October 24, 2021. https://www.chhs.ca.gov/office-of-the-california-surgeon-general/.

Centers for Disease Control and Prevention. "Help Youth at Risk for ACEs." Violence Prevention, Last reviewed April 6, 2021. Accessed October 24, 2021. https://www.cdc.gov/violenceprevention/aces/help-youth-at-risk.html.

Kennedy, Anna Brendle. "Healing Mind and Body from Childhood Trauma: Understanding ACEs." LinkedIn, April 16, 2018. https://www.linkedin.com/pulse/healing-mind-body-from-childhood-trauma-understanding-anna/.

CHAPTER 2—BODY AUTONOMY

Christian, Kayti. "Let's Talk Bodily Autonomy: What It Is & Why We Need It." The Good Trade: Self. Accessed October 24, 2021. https://www.thegoodtrade.com/features/reclaiming-body-autonomy-for-women.

Darkness to Light. "Child Sexual Abuse Statistics: The Magnitude of the Problem." Updated December 22, 2015. Accessed August 28, 2021. http://www.d2l.org/wp-content/uploads/2017/01/Statistics_1_Magnitude.pdf.

Nienow, Shalon MD. "Seven Steps to Teaching Children Body Autonomy." Kite Insights: Safety. Rady Children's Hospital—San Diego website. Accessed October 24, 2021. https://www.rchsd.org/2019/12/seven-steps-to-teaching-children-body-autonomy/.

Sex Positive Families, LLC. (@sexpositive_families). "When adults demand affection from kids, it sends the message that a child's body is an object for other's pleasure, not their own. Here's why that's dangerous." Instagram, May 16, 2020. https://www.instagram.com/p/CAP6pLFJCLs/.

CHAPTER 3—THE BLEACHER REPORT

Leon, Joel. "For Colored Boys Contemplating Suicide." Medium. October 24, 2017. Accessed October 25, 2021. https://level.medium.com/for-colored-boys-contemplating-suicide-6528631828aa.

MOSAC (Mothers of Sexually Abused Children). "Dissociation." Child Sexual Abuse: Long Term Consequences, Accessed October 25, 2021. www.mosac.net/Dissociation.aspx.

Opening the Circle. "Myths and Stereotypes." Defining Abuse, Accessed October 25, 2021. www.openingthecircle.ca/defining-abuse/myths-stereotypes.

The Twelve Project. "About Kevin." About, Accessed October 25, 2021. https://www.thetwelveproject.com/about.

The Twelve Project. "About Us." Accessed October 25, 2021.
www.thetwelveproject.com.

CHAPTER 4—BRUTE FORCE

Child USA. "Delayed Disclosure: A Factsheet Based on Cutting-Edge Research on
Child Sex Abuse." March 2020.
https://childusa.org/wp-content/uploads/2020/04/Delayed-Disclosure-
Factsheet-2020.pdf.

Darkness to Light. "Grooming and Red Flag Behaviors." Take Action: Understand
the Issue, Accessed October 25, 2021.
https://www.d2l.org/child-grooming-signs-behavior-awareness/.

Jeglic, Elizabeth L. PhD. "What Parents Need to Know about Sexual Grooming."
Psychology Today, January 16, 2019. Accessed October 25, 2021.
https://www.education.vic.gov.au/school/teachers/health/childprotection/Pages/
expolitationgrooming.aspx.

CHAPTER 5—ARTIFICIAL INTELLIGENCE

Defend Innocence. "Concerning Behavior: Five Facts About Child on Child Sexual
Abuse (COCSA)." Child Sexual Abuse Risk Reduction: Sexual Development at All
Ages. Accessed October 25, 2021.
https://defendinnocence.org/child-sexual-abuse-risk-reduction/sexual-
development-at-all-ages/concerning-behavior/5-facts-child-child-sexual-abuse/.

Defend Innocence. "Our Mission." About Us, Accessed October 25, 2021.
https://defendinnocence.org/about-us/.

Leftley, Nick. "Kissing Cousins to the Kiss of Death: The Story Behind Every Kissing
Expression." Dollar Shave Club: Timewasters. Accessed September 4, 2021.
https://www.dollarshaveclub.com/content/tag/timewasters/page/19.

CHAPTER 6—PEER REVIEW

Benazir, Citra. "Silent No More." September 7, 2020, in Pleasure Girls Podcast.
Podcast. 16:59.
https://www.listennotes.com/podcasts/pleasure-girls-podcast-citra-benazir-
CAZjRLevuPD/.

Girl Table. "Citra Benazir." The GT Story Project: W. Founder. Accessed October 25, 2021.
https://www.girltable.com/gtstoryproject-wfounder/2020/3/2/citra-benazir.

Shafe, S. and G. Hutchinson. "Child Sexual Abuse and Continuous Influence of Cultural
Practices: A Review." West Indian Medical Journal 63, no. 6 (October 2014): 634–37.
https://www.ncbi.nlm.nih.gov/pmc/articles/PMC4663956/.

Tabachnick, Joan. "Do Children Sexually Abuse Other Children?" Stop It Now!
Accessed October 25, 2021.
https://www.stopitnow.org/sites/default/files/documents/files/do_children_
sexually_abuse_other_children_0.pdf.

CHAPTER 7—MASQUERADING

Davis, Shavontana "Starr." "Why My Law Degree Is Ancillary to My Purpose." *State Bar of Georgia Young Lawyers Division: The YLD Review* 62, no. 2 (March 2021). https://www.gabar.org/newsandpublications/yldnewsletter/upload/62_2.pdf.

Gideon's Promise Inc. "Mission." Accessed October 25, 2021. https://www.gideonspromise.org/about/.

Herman Law. "Lawyers for Clergy Sexual Abuse." Practice Areas: Clergy. Accessed October 25, 2021. https://hermanlaw.com/practices/clergy/clergy-sex-abuse/.

Nemours Kids Health. "Talking to Your Child about Puberty." Kids Health: Parents. Accessed October 25, 2021. https://kidshealth.org/en/parents/talk-about-puberty.html.

Rezendes, Michael. "Church Allowed Abuse by Priest for Years." *Boston Globe*, January 6, 2002. https://www.bostonglobe.com/news/special-reports/2002/01/06/church-allowed-abuse-priest-for-years/cSHfGkTIrAT25qKGvBuDNM/story.html.

CHAPTER 8—COMPRESSION

Centers for Disease Control and Prevention. "Sexual Violence Is Preventable." Injury Prevention & Control, Last reviewed April 19, 2021. Accessed October 25, 2021. https://www.cdc.gov/injury/features/sexual-violence/index.html.

Southern Connecticut State University. "Rape Culture, Victim Blaming, and the Facts." Inside Southern: Sexual Misconduct. Accessed October 25, 2021. https://inside.southernct.edu/sexual-misconduct/facts.

W. Tasha. "I Am Tasha W." Accessed October 25, 2021. https://www.lifewithtashaw.com/.

CHAPTER 9—TREE TRAVERSAL

Clark, Carla. "Homosexuality Link to Child Sex Abuse Confirmed—Gender Nonconformity." Brain Blogger: Psychology & Psychiatry, November 21, 2016. Accessed October 25, 2021. http://www.brainblogger.com/2016/11/21/homosexuality-link-to-child-sex-abuse-confirmed-gender-nonconformity/.

Elite Tree Care, LLC. "Root Rot." Tree Disease Library, Accessed October 25, 2021. https://www.elitetreecare.com/library/tree-diseases/root-rot/.

Hill, Tamara. "How Intergenerational Trauma Impacts Families." Psych Central. April 21, 2020. https://psychcentral.com/blog/caregivers/2018/06/inter-generational-trauma-6-ways-it-affects-families#1.

CHAPTER 10—LOOPING

K12 Academics. "History of Child Sexual Abuse." Sexual Abuse: Child Sexual Abuse, Accessed October 25, 2021. https://www.k12academics.com/sexual-abuse/child-sexual-abuse/history.

Lawson, David. "Understanding and Treating Survivors of Incest." Counseling Today, March 6, 2018. Accessed October 25, 2021. https://ct.counseling.org/2018/03/understanding-treating-survivors-incest/

RAINN (Rape, Abuse & Incest National Network). "Types of Sexual Violence: Incest." Sexual Violence, Accessed October 25, 2021. https://www.rainn.org/articles/incest.

CHAPTER 11—PRIVILEGE ESCALATION
Birthday Wishes Expert. "What to Avoid When Bringing Children Up | 101 Quotes About Bad Parents." Last modified April 12, 2021. Accessed October 26, 2021. https://www.birthdaywishes.expert/bad-parents-quotes/.

Hopper, Jim PhD. "Child Abuse: Recovered Memories of Sexual Abuse." *Jim Hopper.* Accessed October 26, 2021. https://www.jimhopper.com/topics/child-abuse/recovered-memories-of-sexual-abuse/.

M. Meghan. "Reactive Abuse: What It Is and Why Abusers Rely on It." *Break the Silence Against Domestic Violence (BTSADV).* January 28, 2019. Accessed October 26, 2021. https://breakthesilencedv.org/reactive-abuse-what-it-is-and-why-abusers-rely-on-it/?cn-reloaded=1.

Young, Karen. "Breaking the Cycle of Toxic Parenting: How to Silence Old Toxic Messages for Good." *Hey Sigmund,* Accessed October 26, 2021. https://www.heysigmund.com/breaking-the-cycle-of-toxic-parenting/.

CHAPTER 12—BIT MANIPULATION
Letourneau, Elizabeth J. PhD, Luciana C. Assini-Meytin, PhD, Keith L. Kaufman, PhD, Ben Mathews, PhD, and Donald Palmer, PhD. *Preventing and Addressing Child Sexual Abuse in Youth Serving Organizations: A Desk Guide for Organizational Leaders.* Baltimore, MD: Moore Center for the Prevention of Child Sexual Abuse, Johns Hopkins Bloomberg School of Public Health: Moore Center for the Prevention of Child Sexual Abuse, 2020. https://americanhealth.jhu.edu/sites/default/files/2020-11/YSO-Desk-Guide.pdf.

National Council for Curriculum and Assessment. "Identity and Belonging." *Aistear: The Early Childhood Curriculum Framework.* Dublin, Ireland: NCCA, 2009. https://curriculumonline.ie/getmedia/484bcc30-28cf-4b24-90c8-502a868bb53a/Aistear-Principles-and-Themes_EN.pdf

Nelson, Libby. "Grab 'em by the pussy: how Trump talked about women in private is horrifying." Vox, October 7, 2016. Accessed October 26, 2021. https://www.vox.com/2016/10/7/13205842/trump-secret-recording-women.

RAINN (Rape, Abuse & Incest National Network). "Understanding Consent: What Consent Looks Like." Sexual Violence, Accessed October 26, 2021. https://www.rainn.org/articles/what-is-consent.

Relman, Eliza. "The 26 Women Who have Accused Trump of Sexual Misconduct." *Business Insider,* September 17, 2020. https://www.businessinsider.com/women-accused-trump-sexual-misconduct-list-2017.

Stop It Now! "Understanding What Makes Kids Vulnerable to Being Sexually Abused." Accessed October 26, 2021. https://www.stopitnow.org/ohc-content/understanding-what-makes-kids-vulnerable-to-being-sexually-abused.

CHAPTER 13—PRESSURE MODULATION

C.D. Moody Construction. "History." *About.* Accessed October 26, 2021. https://cdmoodyconstruction.com/about/.

Center for Deployment Psychology. "Stuck Point Help Sheet for CPT Therapists." Uniformed Services University, Accessed November 26, 2021. https://deploymentpsych.org/system/files/member_resource/Stuck_Point_Help_Sheet_Therapists.pdf.

Darkness to Light. "Stewards of Children®." *Take Action: Get Trained,* Accessed October 26, 2021. https://www.d2l.org/education/stewards-of-children/

Henry, Terry. "How Can I Earn the Trust of My Spouse if They've Suffered Childhood Abuse?" TheHopeLine: Accessed October 26, 2021. thehopeline.com.

Jazeb, Melody. "'Cognitive Processing Therapy and 'Stuck Points' that prevent healing from Trauma." *Cognitive Behavior Therapy Center of Southern California,* November 1, 2019. https://cbtsocal.com/cognitive-processing-therapy-and-stuck-points-that-prevent-healing-from-trauma/.

Moody Speaks. "Meet David." *About.* Accessed October 26, 2021. https://moodyspeaks.com/about/.

CHAPTER 14—THE PROGRAMMER

Gray, Emma. "11 Ways Maya Angelou Taught Us to Be Better Women." *HuffPost,* May 28, 2014. Accessed October 26, 2021. https://www.huffpost.com/entry/maya-angelou-women-quotes_n_5404284.

CHAPTER 15—REVERSE ENGINEERING ABUSE

Brown, Brené. "About." *Brené Brown LLC,* 2021. https://brenebrown.com/about/.

THE ADVERSE CHILDHOOD EXPERIENCES QUESTIONNAIRE

American Society for the Positive Care of Children. "Take the ACEs Quiz." Learning Center: Adverse Childhood Experiences, Accessed October 29, 2021. https://americanspcc.org/take-the-aces-quiz/.